One of the best books written within the men's liberation movement, and without doubt the most personal.
—**Francis Baumli**, Ph.D., representative to the National Coalition of Free Men

For women and men who truly seek an equality between the sexes this book will be an inspiration.
—Pacific Sun

As more people read Mr. Diamond's invaluable book, fewer will require expensive counseling.
—**George M. Soule**, M.D., San Diego, California.

Sensitive, honest, courageous, and beautiful!
—**Fred Hayward**, President, Men's Rights, Inc.

It's as if the therapist you might seek out switches roles with you, lays on the couch and tells YOU the intimate details of HIS own journey.
—**Robert Rimmer**, author of The Harrad Experiment

Pioneers in the explicitness and candor of its first-person narrative in exploring an age.
—Stockton Record

The only book to show men how to approach women as loving equals.
—**Dr. James E. Brogan**, Professor of English, San Francisco State University.

INSIDE OUT

Becoming My Own Man

Jed Diamond

© 1983 Jed Diamond

published by Fifth Wave Press
P.O. Box 9355
San Raphael, CA 94912

typesetting and pasteup by
Whatever Bookworks
158 E. Blithedale
Mill Valley, CA 94941

editing by Mark Allen
cover design by John Goodchild
cover painting by Jen-Ann Kirchmeier
back cover photo by Lawrence Ross

Acknowledgments

For the many people who have participated in the various stages of this book's birth process.

Carlin Diamond • Mark Allen • Edith Diamond

Richard Baltzell • John Bandy • Tony Black • Dan
Blake • Robert Bly • Sherran Boll • Jim
Brogan • Norman Brown • Arthur
Coleman • Dick Fireman • Betty Friedan • Jack
Gibb • Theonie Gilmore • Herb Goldberg • Ruth
Gottstein • Debra Hudson • Sam Julty • Bob
Larzelere • Kellie Layne • Shirley
Luthman • Deena Metzger • Paul Mico • Pierre
Mornell • Tom Mosmiller • Steven
Muchnick • Phil Muir • Ken Petron • Hugh
Prather • Dick Ridenour • Robert Rimmer • John
Robinson • Natalie Rogers • Lawrence Ross • Bob
Sayers • Jonathan Sharpe • Larry
Sherridan • Tom Sipes • David Steinberg • Dave
Thompson • Stephen Vincent

Contents

Opening

We played together like three little kids, my wife, my friend, and me. We laughed and joked, went out to eat, had ice cream together. It felt like a family, playing with the brother and sister I never had. When Lindy suggested we all go camping together I was excited to deepen our family ties. I wasn't prepared for the pain of what followed.

We found a campsite and spent time lying out in the sun and walking along the river. Later in the afternoon Lindy and I got into one of our philosophical discussions about "open marriage" and what it would be like if we were sexual with someone else. Maybe someday it would be right for us.

"I hope you'll let me know if you and Lenn ever decide you want to be sexual." Like in 20 years or so I thought to myself.

"We do," said Lindy brightly.

"Oh really," I said calmly, feeling like I'd just been kicked in the balls. "Well, let's talk about it."

Lenn arrived and the sharing began. They both wanted to make love with each other, but didn't want to hurt or threaten me. I admitted that even though we'd been talking about it for some time, I was shocked and fearful of the reality of the situation. But on the other hand, I felt this might be the time to experience the reality of what we'd been talking about for so long. We'd been feeling like one big family and maybe this was the time to extend the sharing to sexual intimacy.

Lenn left us alone and Lindy and I walked and talked. She seemed so loving and supportive. I really felt her love for me and her desire not to hurt me. She said she felt ready to open up our relationship and have sex with Lenn. She felt it would enhance our relationship and not hurt it. The more we talked, the more open and expansive I felt. My fears gradually calmed down.

We agreed that I would stay with the kids in the tent and she and Lenn would spend some time in the woods, and then Lindy would return and spend the rest of the night with me. It all seemed so romantic and noble. "Dutiful, liberated husband stays with the children while wife and friend make love in the woods. She returns after 20 minutes to say it was nice but doesn't at all compare with making love with you. Husband and wife make mad, passionate love the rest of the night, and the three friends walk off into the sunrise the next morning."

In the tent alone I found my heart pounding wildly. "I'm not sure I made the right decision, but there's no turning back now. I'll practice the new meditation I just learned and it will be over soon. Lindy will be back here with me and our relationship will be firmer and more loving than it has ever been."

The night was quiet and dark, the tent was warm and cozy and I felt comfortable hearing the children quietly breathing. But then I began to hear sounds from outside, quiet at first, then louder. "Oh God I can hear them. She's getting fucked and loving it. I'm scared. I'm going to lose her. She'll want to stay with him and won't want to come back to me."

But then it quieted down, except for my heart which I couldn't seem to slow down. In just a little more time and I'd be OK and it would be over. "Shit, there it is again. She's calling out his name. Please God, make it stop. Make it go away. Make me not hear it" . . . Quiet again. "How long has it been? Has it been 20 minutes or two hours? She's got to come back to me *now*."

I heard them again, the screams, the moans, and it was driving me *crazy*. I couldn't stand it anymore. All I could see was my wife slipping away, and I was a little boy again and my mother was in the next room and I heard them making love and I knew she was going to leave me and run off with him, and I was going to die.

"They're trying to drive me crazy and I've got to get out of here. I've got to get away from the sounds. I've got to make them stop. But I can't. If I go out and stop them I'll never know if she would have come back and if I break my agreement to wait here I'll lose her for sure. God, more sounds, over and over and over. Won't it ever stop? Oh God, please stop them, please, please, *please. .*"

But it didn't stop and I had to do something or go mad. I ran out of the tent in the dark calling, "Lindy, Lindy, I can't take it anymore. Please help me." They called to me from the dark and I followed her voice to their love nest, sobbing uncontrollably. They scrambled into their clothes and Lindy held me close. I felt safe. But then I realized I was in the middle of their love space and the place smelled of sweat and sex and I wanted to spit on them and leave. But I didn't have the guts and I hated myself for my weakness.

We sat together in the back seat of the car, three lost souls, each wrapped in our own thoughts, facing the grey morning.

Introduction

The summer after I turned 27 I felt I had the world by the tail. Lindy and I had been married five years; Gene, our son, was two years old; we'd recently bought a three-bedroom house, the culmination of a long-held dream. I felt I was reaching the height of my career. I was director of the county drug abuse programs, had recently published my first paper in a professional journal, was on the faculty of two colleges, and was well-liked and respected by my collegues.

Even though the twin pillars in my dream, a loving family and a successful career, seemed well in place, I felt uneasy. I was beginning to notice the first rumblings of change and I didn't understand them. It seemed I'd gotten everything I went after since I graduated from college six years before, and yet I was afraid.

Ten years later my life had changed dramatically. The two solid pillars, which had seemed everlasting, had crumbled. New ones had been built and others added. The Women's Movement first helped me question the roles we had all built our lives upon. It stimulated a desire to have the support of men who were going through similar changes. I joined a men's group and received tremendous support and insight.

I looked hungrily for books on Men's Liberation and was delighted when I found one, and disappointed and angered to see the number of women's books grow larger and the number of books on men's changes remain so limited. I wanted to read books by men that talked of their personal struggles, their actual hopes and dreams, marriages and divorces, career successes and failures, their love for their children, and their feelings for their friends.

I wanted to know about the real changes men go through, not the theoretical passages that look so easy on paper, but feel so different when they are lived out. I wondered if I was the only one who was unclear about what it was to be a man. What I learned when I was growing up seemed confused. John Wayne and Clint Eastwood seemed clear about what a "real" man was, but they didn't fit my sense of self. Besides, Women's Lib and all the women I knew denounced the macho male and had their own definition of a "real" man, always powerful and always sensitive, forever strong and also gentle. This seemed closer to my image of the ideal man and worth working towards. It took me years to realize that trying to live this image was also doomed to failure.

This book is a chronicle of my own process of understanding what it means to become a man. I see my search as an on-going process, rather than having reached any kind of end point, since there never is a point at which we can say, "We have arrived, the journey has ended, now I am complete, now I am a man." I've chosen to share a great deal about my own personal journey because I believe that through our personal sharing with each other we can find our own unique path towards wholeness.

Inside Out is more than a personal statement. I've also tried to share my understanding of the various stages that men go through in their journey in search of themselves. This understanding has evolved from both my own process as well as from my work over the last 17 years as a therapist working with men and women, individually and in relationship. What has stood out for me as a therapist over the years is the tremendous hunger both men and women have to understand what men are experiencing in moving through adulthood in the 80's. Much of the turmoil many couples experience in their relationships stems from this lack of understanding and from the fear, guilt, and anger that results when people blame each other for a process they don't understand.

Although the book addresses itself to men's issues, it is not a book for men only. I believe that women are vitally interested in understanding men's experience. They too wonder if they are alone in breaking out of old constraints and finding new pathways to fulfillment. They would like to believe that men are also seeking new answers, but they find it difficult to connect with the emerging man's experience. I feel a connection with women in another way as well: My hope is that women will read the book and relate to my story in the same way I related to much of what I first read in feminist literature. Beyond gender differences we are all human and our struggles are ultimately more similar than different.

I've been told by some people that what I have said is too personal, and that I should fictionalize the characters. I've not been willing to do that. I've changed the names and settings only to the degree that it will protect the privacy of people who do not wish their lives to be shared so broadly. I feel good in sharing about myself, to let others know that their changes and struggles are not so fearful and unique. I feel we all have a great deal to learn about becoming more fully human. I have certainly learned much more in the process of sharing myself, and not hiding behind a fictional character.

Inside Out is a book to be read with your whole being, not just your intellect. I encourage you to open yourself to your feelings, to your hopes and dreams as well as your fears. Allow yourself to let the words act as triggers for your own experience of growth, your own sense of understanding of what it means to be human. I don't want to offer another "ideal" image to strive for, but rather to share a process of growth to stimulate your search within for your own being.

Chapter One

I Am Taught What I Am

The Images I Grew Up With

I remember when I was about three years old, riding on my dad's shoulders while he walked through a park in Encino, California. I was wildly happy, sitting on the top of the world watching the blue skys and billowy white clouds. Endless miles of citrus orchards spread out in all directions around the park. Dad seemed free and without cares, occasionally whistling a lullaby and throwing peanuts to the pigeons. Mom was home doing typing for one of the soon-to-be blacklisted novelists. No one ever told me but I knew that the reason she worked was because Dad wasn't making any money, although he tried desperately hard to sell his stories to the emerging television industry in the Hollywood of the 40's.

My next strong memory was when I was five and Mom told me that Dad was going into a hospital. She tried to explain that it had something to do with his nerves, but I didn't understand. I just knew that he was gone and Mom and I were alone. My uncle would take me to visit him every Sunday. I always knew we were getting close to the hospital when we passed between the huge Eucalyptus trees that lined the road just outside of Camarillo. At first Dad didn't seem very interested in me and then he didn't seem to know who I was. We finally stopped going.

From the few things my mom said, filtered through my five-year-old mind, I "knew" the reason he had gotten sick and gone away was because the responsibilities of bringing up a child and making a living were too much. I remember seeing pictures of my mom and dad, dressed in their winter coats in New York before I was born. I knew Dad was happy then. Things were fine until I came along. I knew too that the signs of collapse were his excitement and joy which seemed to precede his times of unhappiness and fear.

My mother learned to drive and continued to take in work so our little family could survive. She seemed to do it much more easily than my dad, and I learned early that women were the real strength in a family.

My dad was in Camarillo State Hospital six months before they let him out for a weekend visit. I was staying with some friends at their house when he came looking for me. I wanted to run and see him, but my mom told me to stay inside while she and her friend went out to talk with him. The way she told me to go inside frightened me and all three of us kids hid under the bed. The oldest one told me that if my dad hurt her mother, she would kill me. The women returned an hour later unharmed and announced that he had left. It was clear that my father had become not only sick but dangerous.

No one else in the neighborhood had an absent father and it seemed that all Dads worked and Moms stayed home to watch the kids. I heard a rumor from other kids that Carolyn's father was "out of work" but I didn't really believe it until I heard my mother talking to other women in the neighborhood, their voices a mixture of pity and contempt. Rudy had been out of work a month and Beth had been forced to take in typing as my mom had. The worst part, according to Beth, was having to put up with Rudy moping around the house. Tears came to my eyes and I felt scared and angry. I made a promise to myself that I would never turn out like Rudy.

The Fears That Drive Me

The early experiences I had with my family created a number of fears that drove me for many years. To put them into a simple list:

1. My feelings will destroy me if I let them.

2. I'll go crazy like my father.
3. I'll be a failure at work and lose my family's respect.
4. There's something dangerous and violent in me waiting to destroy the people I love the most.
5. Women will "love" me, but underneath the surface, they'll feel pity and contempt.

The Commandments That Move Me*

1. Thou shalt not be weak, nor have weak gods before thee.
2. Thou shalt not fail thyself, nor "fail" as thy father before thee.
3. Thou shalt not keep holy any day that denies thy work.
4. Thou shalt not express strong emotions, neither high nor low.
5. Thou shalt not cry, complain, or ask for help.
6. Thou shalt not be hostile or angry, especially towards loved ones.
7. Thou shalt not be uncertain or ambivalent.
8. Thou shalt not be dependent.
9. Thou shalt not acknowledge thy death or thy limitations.
10. Thou *shalt* do unto other men before they do unto you.

The "Real" Man of the 60's . . .
But My World Changed in 1956

I was 13 years old in 1956, an important age in Jewish tradition. Although my upbringing was not religious, I did feel a special responsibility beyond myself as I approached "manhood." Growing up I felt I walked in two worlds. I seemed to truly understand the world of my parents. I would listen for hours on end to an album they had, called "Manhattan Towers," which described the world of New

*Revised from an unpublished article by Dick Vittitow.

17

York, the world they had grown up in and lived in. I also felt connected to the world of my peers, the music and the dances, the cars and customs. I believed those that said we were at a crossroads in human history, that we were moving from an old civilization to a new one. I truly felt that I was at a crossroads in history, at the beginning of a new age.

In 1956 the "old" civilization was at its peak. Eisenhower had been elected for a second term as President. Liberace was playing to world-wide acclaim. The $64,000 Question and the Ed Sullivan Show were the top-rated TV programs. Billy Graham's popularity heralded a resurgence in traditional religion. The U.S. economic system was at its peak. President Harlow Herbert Curtice of General Motors was named Man of the Year.

If the preceding reflected the civilization at its peak, there were also indicators of the "new" civilization to come. Twenty-one-year-old Elvis "The Pelvis" Presley was sought after by Ed Sullivan despite his previous vow that he would not have the gyrating groaner "at any price" on his family TV show. Miltown became the latest and most popular tranquilizing drug, and began a popular shift toward "altered states of consciousness." Said Milton Berle in 1956, "It's worked wonders for me. In fact, I'm thinking of changing my name to Miltown Berle." That same year, Alfred Kinsey died, amid increasing interest in his work on human sexuality.

Women's change in status was marked in significant ways that year. For the first time in history, women stockholders outnumbered men among the eight-million U.S. shareholders. In searching for a safe, effective birth control pill, the words of Margaret Sanger who started Planned Parenthood proclaimed, "No woman can consider herself free until she can determine the number of children she will have." The Pill was perfected for public use by G.D. Searle Company in 1956.

Time Magazine reported that "both North and South Vietnam, formerly part of French Indochina, were granted their independence from France in July 1954, under terms of the Geneva Agreements which stipulated that free elections would be held on July 20, 1956 for the purpose of uniting the two countries. But President Ngo Dinh Diem of South Vietnam refused to abide by the election agreement on the grounds that Communists in the North intended to prevent a fair election. Both the U.S.. and Great Britain sided with Diem." As I reached draft age, I felt profoundly influenced by that decision.

Another change, more subtle but potentially more profound than all the rest, also occurred that same year. The United States became the first major power in which more than 50 percent of the labor force ceased to be on the farms or in the factories, but were now in such occupations as retail trade, communications, research, education, and other service categories.

Human beings had spent four million years concentrating on their needs for physical survival and safety. For the first time in history, a large number of human beings had their basic needs met and could concentrate on meeting needs for self-esteem, prestige, belongingness, love, and self-development. I knew, early on, I had to learn to meet these needs and help my loved ones meet them as well.

I'd always felt extreme conflict trying to understand how to live in a "new" world with deeply held values and beliefs, many of which I had learned in the "old" world.

My heroes while growing up were Paul Newman, Robert Mitchum, and Gary Cooper. Even though Newman and Mitchum were great, I was most profoundly influenced by the Gary Cooper I saw in "High Noon." I saw "High Noon" more times than any other movie before or since, and I loved going to movies. Coop was the ultimate hero. He exemplified strength and dignity. He was tall, soft-spoken, and absolutely clear about what was important in life. A woman's love was basically important. But more important than that was to keep his word and do his job in the world of men. I still remember the theme song from the movie. "Do not forsake me, oh my darling . . . . Look at that big hand move along, nearing High Noon . . . I'm not afraid of death but, oh, what would I do if you leave me?" And she was clear that she was going to leave if he put on his guns to fight that crazy fight with no purpose. But I knew even then that a man's gotta do what he's gotta do, or face the ultimate failure: to "lie a coward, a craven coward, in his grave."

For months afterwards (probably years and years), I practiced walking tall, pretending I had a beauty waiting for me when my work was done, always careful not to do anything which might mark me as a coward and separate me forever from the "real" world.

Chapter Two

I Live Out What I Am

Entering the Adult World

Until I was a senior in high school, I had always wanted to be a "businessman" when I grew up, mainly because that's what my mother was, or at least all the men she worked with were. When I was a senior, I got A's on all the physiology exams given by Mr. Gray, considered the most demanding teacher in the entire school. I didn't like physiology much, but I liked to memorize and Mr. Gray encouraged my "interest." I liked the praise of a man I respected and when I went off to college the next year, I put down my major as "pre-med."

I was as good in college as I had been in high school and carried a 3.7 average into my senior year when I began applying to medical schools, though I enjoyed anthropology, psychology, and sociology a great deal more than quantititive analysis, organic chemistry, or the other "pre-med" classes. I didn't know if I really wanted to be a doctor, but I liked the sound of "Doctor" better than anything else I could think of, and my mom and friends all seemed excited at the prospect of having a doctor close at hand.

I had never dated through high school, convinced that no girl I would be interested in could possibly be interested in me. Even my shyest friends got dates for the senior all-night party, but I found reasons to stay at home and read.

When I went off to college, 150 miles from home, I figured no one would know I was petrified of girls, and I "pretended" I knew what I was doing. Much to my surprise, the girls didn't seem to know that I didn't know what I was doing, and my college years were full of female social contact. Most all the girls I dated dutifully held off my sexual advances, and the few that didn't scared the wits out of me and I stopped for fear that they might get pregnant. In those days, that was a good enough reason to stop and I never had to explore my own fears of sexual intimacy.

I met Lindy at a scholarship dinner when I was a senior and she was a freshman. I was 21 and she was 18. She seemed to be everything I wasn't: free and a little crazy, emotional, worldly, and seemingly wise, and most of all she seemed to be as entranced with me as I was with her. I spent the following summer in Miami with her before my planned entrance into medical school in the fall.

My summer was free and exciting. Lindy had started using birth control pills to "regulate her menstrual flow" and it seemed natural to move our sexual exploration ahead to include intercourse. I still felt scared the first time, worrying about whether I'd do it right or if anyone would catch us, but it went OK. We enjoyed many warm summer evenings sneaking outside her house and making love in the back yard.

We were in love and life seemed so easy. As C.P. Snow said, "When two people are under the influence of the most violent, most insane, most delusive, and most transient of passions, they are required to swear that they will remain in that excited, abnormal, and exhausting condition continuously until death do they part." Neither of us had ever heard of Snow at the time. We planned to be married the following June.

Living Out the Dream

I began medical school in the fall and Lindy returned to continue her studies at U.C. Santa Barbara. We talked daily on the phone, found ingenius ways to call person-to-person for the likes of "Ima Misanue" and get a message through without paying for it.

Medical school was a shock for me. Everyone was terrified, sure they weren't going to make it, and they were going to make damn sure that if someone went it was you and not them. Everyone seemed to get totally blitzed on the weekends in between cramming themselves full of "facts" about parts of the anatomy. Those of us on scholarships were taken on the first weekend to visit the home of one of our professors in the hills of Marin County. The message I got was "stay clean, don't rock the boat while you're here, and this too will be yours someday." As a child of social activist parents, I was appalled. This did not seem to be my ideal of lofty medical practitioners making the world healthier and happier for the poor and downtrodden.

I didn't sleep the first two weeks of school, although I looked fine to those around me. I didn't know I was just as terrified as the rest of my cohorts. I hid my fear behind calm smiles. Two weeks after classes began, in the middle of my histology class, I closed my microscope case, walked out of class, and told the Dean I had decided to quit medical school. He asked if anything was wrong. I said no, I had just decided to leave and go into social work (the only "reasonable" thing I could think to say). He seemed agreeable but said I needed to see one other person before I could leave. It turned out to be a psychiatrist who came in on her off day from her office in Marin.

I said nothing of my sleeplessness nor my fears, just shared my new-found desire to go into social work. She asked me a few questions, was pleasant, but since I was obviously not psychotic I was given the OK to leave. It was clear that a lot of people felt someone must be crazy to leave medical school after three weeks and give back a four-year, full tuition scholarship, and she encouraged me to return when I came to my senses.

I transferred to U.C. Berkeley and began graduate school in social work. Lindy and I were married in June as planned, and I began seeing a psychiatrist at the student health center to find out why I had done such an obviously irrational thing as dropping out of medical school, even though it felt right. I never found out while seeing that psychiatrist, but it turned out I liked social work very much. I liked learning about the psychological, interpersonal, and social aspects of people better than the purely physical.

Berkeley in 1965 was a campus awash with excitement. The Free Speech Movement the year before had laid the foundation for the Viet Nam protests. I was clearly against the war, but very frightened that I would be drafted and have to decide whether to fight, go to jail, or leave the country. At noon, I attended the protest rallies. After school, I went to all the recruiting stations trying to see if I could join some part of the service where I wouldn't have to fight (or die). I found out I wouldn't even be safe in the Coast Guard, and as to my concern about wearing glasses, the recruiter assured me they could fit my gas mask with the proper lenses.

Through the months of fear and indecision, I began to develop my own convictions about the war. I knew I didn't want to die, but then it became clear that I could not support others dying or killing either. I decided I would not be drafted and would leave the country or go to jail if that was the choice. Lindy was supportive and I realized that much of my desire to marry was to have someone special to be with and support me during difficult times like those were.

I ended up being classified 4-F because of an asthma condition, which was fine with me. I completed my graduate studies and began working at Napa State Hospital.

My first "real" job was on a mixed psychiatric unit with people having a range of problems from depression, to mania, to drug abuse, to fears of being drafted. I felt drawn to the younger people, most of whom had drug and alcohol problems, and although I had little direct experience myself, I seemed to relate well with them. A new program was forming to do something different with "drug problems" and somehow I emerged as the new director.

Four years after we were married, Lindy and I had the son we had hoped for. Gene was born, using the LaMaze method, with me present helping Lindy with her breathing during the 22 hours she was in labor. As I watched Gene come into the world, I was overcome with a joy and a rapture I had never before experienced. Tears poured down my cheeks as I held him for the first time, feeling terribly grateful I had let Lindy talk me into going through the birth process together.

The following years were golden. My world was complete. I continued to advance in my career and expand my areas of influence. Our family was growing and our marriage was solid. Gene was healthy and happy and we had just enough friends to round out our social interests.

First Fears

"I want to drive back to South Dakota with Dena, what do you think?" Lindy was brimming over with excitement. She really wanted to go on this trip with her girlfriend. My hesitation lasted only a split second, drowned easily by my desire to please and to prove to myself I was a "liberated" husband.

"Sure, that's fine with me. It will give me a chance to be with Gene." They left the next day, amidst hugs and kisses and a few tears. Gene, just two years old, waved as they drove away.

The day went fine. We wrestled and played, talked about dinner and how fun it was to have just the two men together. It wasn't until Gene had finally fallen off to sleep, after two stories and a rather unusual rendition of Brahm's Lullaby (it always sounded so nice when my mother sang it), that the fears began to creep in. What will I feed him in the morning? What will I do if he starts crying and I can't get him to stop? What if something happens to Lindy and I'm left with Gene? And somewhere way deep was a fleeting thought, what if she meets someone else and leaves me?

But my rational mind easily took charge. "I'm beyond all that. We've been married six years. I'm a successful therapist, director of the county's drug abuse treatment programs. At 28, I've published two papers in professional journals and have developed a reputation as a skilled and competent administrator. We've both read Rimmer's *Harrad Experiment* and although we're not ready for Open Marriage, I know we can love more than one person when the time comes."

After five days, Lindy returned. The fear had vanished, covered by my new-found competence as a father able to handle a two-year-old, no problem at all! I was only mildly uneasy when Lindy told me about a guy she had talked with and kissed Friday night. She said she had been lonely, missing me, wanting someone to comfort her. She was intensely interested in me sexually, which I liked, and she even wanted to experiment with new techniques. She wanted our lovemaking to last longer and talked about my learning to ejaculate more than once each time we made love. It all sounded great to me.

A week later, I noticed a burning when I pissed, and two weeks later I finally went to a doctor. Dr. Roberts told me I had a urinary tract infrection and prostatitis and gave me some medication. The burning didn't bother me so much, but it felt like my ejaculations weren't as strong as they used to be and it wasn't as enjoyable making love with Lindy. I was glad I had gone to the doctor and felt almost relieved to know I had a physical problem that could be cured.

Four months after Lindy returned from South Dakota, I got a surprise phone call. I'd been so busy at work, I hadn't had time to think about anything else. A call from an Adoptions Agency disturbed the activity of the afternoon. I heard myself saying, "You have a child you think would be right for us?" My heart began pounding. It had been over a year since we had first begun talking about adopting a child. I'd almost forgotten we were still waiting.

"She's black?...when was she born?" I couldn't seem to keep my mind clear. "She was born when? So that would make it... shit I can't even subtract. That would make her two and a-half months old. Her, she's a girl! That's good, we wanted a girl. She's in Los Angeles and we can see her in two days if we want to drive down?"

I was excited but confused. I remembered seven years back when we were still in college and sat on the cliffs overlooking the ocean at Santa Barbara talking about our future. "Let's have one child and adopt one." It all seemed so simple. "We do want one of our own flesh and blood and if there are children in the world who need homes, we should help. And besides, we want a boy and a girl and adopting is a sure way of getting a choice."

I called Lindy, who was immediately ecstatic. She had no doubts and since I couldn't find any logical basis for mine, I dismissed them. Two days later on the way to Los Angeles, the doubts returned. They were vague, nothing I could put my finger on, but very much there. As I began talking about them, rushing down the freeway at 70 miles an hour, I began to cry. I blurted out that I was afraid that if I didn't agree to adopt the baby Lindy would leave me. I knew it was an irrational fear, but it was still hanging on to me. Lindy put out her own fear. If I didn't want the baby it would be because she was black, and since there were only racially mixed children available, she wouldn't ever have the daughter she wanted. I told her I didn't think my concern was because she was black. Lindy reassured me she wouldn't leave me and my fears vanished.

A week later, Sandy joined our family, a little black bundle of joy. Our friends threw a surprise shower for Sandy and she was welcomed into our home with style and love.

My body ached for a long time, for no reason. I felt like shit. I was tired, but I couldn't seem to rest. I tried to talk to Lindy, but she was busy with the kids and had her own problems, and besides she wouldn't really understand the pressures I was under, what I faced day after day in the real world. This was one I'd have to work out for myself. The sky was grey and cold and I didn't feel anything inside.

Seven years before, I had begun graduate school in social work. I had a mission in life. I knew I wanted to make the world better in some little way. I came to the San Joaquin Valley because I felt I could really have an impact on a community. Drugs were a major problem in many people's lives and we could do something about it. I was excited to be working with other people who shared my vision. But now it all felt like a pile of shit. I was just part of another bureaucracy whose real purpose was to perpetuate itself.

Two and one-half years after taking the position as Drug Abuse Program Director, I had been asked to leave, publicly because the job was no longer required, privately because I had alienated too many people suggesting the bureaucracy needed to change. I was transferred back to an outpatient mental health unit.

The "medical model" was very much in vogue there. The patients were seen as having some sort of "disease" — psychosis, neurosis, character disorder, or whatever. Our job was to administer some kind of cure, either through giving medications or through giving them the proper words. In this model the therapists had the magic answers and the patients were the passive recipients of this magic. I used to think that things were that easy, and all we had to do was wave our magic wand and people would get better.

Now my notion had more to do with the idea that the person was the center of activity, not the therapist. People came for help because they no longer believed that they were in charge of their own lives. They felt hopeless and helpless and their symptoms were their best attempts at living in the face of their beliefs that life for them was somehow impossible. My job as a therapist was to use my own being, not some magic tools, to help people regain the courage to look and find the answers inside themselves.

It seemed strange going back to being a social worker/ therapist after having been the County Drug Abuse Program Director. I told myself I wasn't really that hung up on the status and the title, but I guess I was. More than the loss of title was the loss of the dream. I really thought I could help improve the world if I could just get far enough up to see what was going on and have the power to change things. In the "dream" I saw myself well on my way to the top by the time I was 30. Now I felt like I was starting all over again and I didn't even know which direction to look to find the top.

Trading the "Real" Man for the "Liberated" Man

Lenn arrived from the California Men's Colony. My first real client at Napa State Hospital when I began in social work five years before, Lenn was intelligent, articulate, successful. He was known as the cocaine king of the San Francisco Bay Area and was a very good illegal drug manufacturer until he got arrested and sent to prison. I immediately liked Lenn when we first met. He seemed to have an excitement and life about him that radiated all the time.

Where I knew about drugs from textbooks, Lenn knew about them from experience. He told me stories about his life on the streets and his experiences as a "flower child" in San Francisco. I loved his story about meeting people who wanted to score dope in Golden Gate Park. He would take them back to his apartment on Haight Street and instead of selling them dope he would help them decide if they really wanted to continue using. He said he had some success and I believed him. It seemed very much like Lenn to sell drugs and at the same time try to convince kids that it was bad for them.

Lenn would listen to my ideas about drug programs and why people go into the field. "Do you want to know about therapists, Lenn? Let me tell you. We love to get our needs met, often at the expense of the people we are trying to help. We who work with addicts are a special breed of therapists. We love to save the addict that is forever getting into trouble and ruining his life. It's an endless job, but we never tire of trying to save him from himself. We're enmored with what our fantasy tells us is the lifestyle of the addict. We like to get close to the excitement of stealing, drug running, pimping and prostituting, and the indefinable high of the forbidden drugs. In our fantasies, we long to do all the forbidden, exciting things that the addict does. We, of course, are respectable. We can't go slumming but we can be 'helpful'. We can listen to the fantasic stories of lust and violence, even better than television, and do our best to 'understand'. The true professional people-helper lives life vicariously, and drug addicts are a real gold mine of life which can be experienced secondhand. Maybe someday we'll get wise and admit that we lack something that the addict has, some life experience, excitement, the guts to turn on and drop out. When we admit our own needs and take our own responsibility for satisying them, we won't have to live our lives through others. So much for my prejudice against professional helpers. Our guilt is endless and we never tire of beating ourselves."

Lenn would just smile and I'd go on with my harangue. "The whole emphasis in society today on drugs as a problem is misplaced. At a hundred meetings of professionals and public alike, you hear about the drug menace. One year it's LSD, the next it's cocaine, another year, it's marijuana or alcohol. Billions of dollars are spent and politicians are elected who promise to put an end to the problem, and everyone pats themselves on the back for taking action. Meanwhile, children are dying. More and more lives are destroyed and no one seems to know why. They think more money is needed, or stricter rules, or better programs.

"Programs that try to deal with drug problems will spend more and more money while more and more children die on their doorsteps, children begging for help, begging to be seen as human beings, not 'drug problems'. They're asking that we see them and hear them and touch them. But in our terror, all we see is a drug problem.

"If children are dying it is because we have not shown them how to live. We have not demonstrated by our actions that life is worth living. What you see happening is mass suicide. Children are dying because they find no life to sustain them. We teach by our actions that the best way to deal with life's problems is by withdrawing. We withdraw into our evening cocktail or our therapist, or if we're very modern into the sensual experience of our hot-tubs. Having taught them well the beauties of escape we have the audacity to want to create 'drug programs' to take away the only means of escape they have available to them."

Somewhere in the process of our nightly talks, Lenn and I became friends. Lenn had left the hospital and I didn't hear from him again until he was in jail. Lindy and I visited him a few times and helped set up a job for him when he got out. But I wasn't quite ready for the reality of seeing Lenn on our doorstep.

Since early in our marriage Lindy and I had talked about "open marriage." For us the idea of "openness" was a way of expanding our family to include other adults, a way of developing our own extended family. We also acknowledged that we were both sexually drawn to various friends of ours, but neither of us liked the secretive, hidden process of having an affair. We were trying to build a relationship based on honesty and trying to hide our sexual activity didn't seem to fit that ideal. We had both read books about people living in a sexually open relationship and it seemed lovely. Although we didn't know of any of our friends who had actually "done" it, we talked about it a great deal.

Although our marriage seemed solid, I always had a fear that it was too good to last. Someday Lindy would find someone who was better than me and I'd be alone. Open marriage seemed to provide an opportunity to develop our relationship on a firmer basis without the fears that were always lurking just below the surface. I felt I was an innovator at work and I wanted to be one also in relationships. I knew the "real" man ideals I grew up with weren't working, and I felt that the new "liberated" ideals were just the answer.

Lenn's arrival was an opportunity to finally put into practice what I had talked about for so long and the weekend camping trip turned out to be just the opportunity. Though I wasn't prepared for my feelings, after the pain of the night wore off I began to see my feelings as another obstacle to be overcome in my pursuit of my liberated ideal. I had always been good at solving problems as I rose to the top in my profession. Uncomfortable feelings were just additional problems to solve and I was excited to get on with the process.

A week after the camping trip, I returned to the doctor to review progress with my prostatitis. It hadn't seemed to improve, but he gave me some other medication which he assured me would help the problem. On the way back home, I had a spur-of-the-moment idea to have rings made for our seventh anniversary, which was two weeks away. I stopped at a shop in Berkeley and discussed the design. We agreed on a gold band in the shape of intertwined vines, for our relationship continuing forever, with spaces in the

31

design, for our emerging openness. I felt a real excitement about the next seven years of marriage. We had finally acted on all our discussion that it was possible to love more than one person at once, and that jealousy and fear could be overcome with caring and trust.

Lindy and Lenn decided to stop being sexual until I felt more comfortable with it. It was obvious that she hoped my discomfort would go away soon. I felt much better anyway. The memories of the weekend faded quickly away and she seemed so happy with her new involvement with Lenn, I didn't want to say no. I also couldn't seem to shake the fear, even though I knew it was groundless, that Lindy would leave me if I didn't go along with her seeing Lenn. I felt like I'd lost my chance to say no when I agreed it would be OK for them to be sexual on our camping weekend.

Soon things were on again with Lenn and Lindy. I felt OK through the day as long as I kept busy and didn't think about the nights. But when Lindy was away seeing Lenn, I felt like I was being pulled apart. I'd always been so good at figuring things out, at finding the "right" solution to all problems. But I couldn't make any sense out of this one. It seemed right that we should be able to love more than one person, to give to one without taking away from another. There was enough to go around. Books like the *Harrad Experiment* and *Open Marriage* said that people could be open sexually without damaging their relationship. I also believed that jealousy was based on fear and insecurity and could be overcome. I wanted that kind of freedom for Lindy and for myself. And yet when she was gone I would shake inside. I couldn't seem to concentrate on anything. I re- played the weekend camping trip over and over in my mind. I couldn't seem to forget and I couldn't seem to get passed it. I tortured myself and I couldn't seem to stop. If only I had said "no" from the beginning or suggested they be sexual at a time when I wasn't around.

I wanted so much to move to a new level of loving and freedom with Lindy. I knew I could make it work. It would just take time for the jealousy and anger to go away. It was so clear in my mind, but my body wasn't there yet. My body would draw back from Lindy when we made love. She seemed dirty and cheap to me now. I hated feeling like that. I felt dirty and cheap myself, just like all the fucking chauvinist men I knew. "I'm better than that. *I'm fucking better than that...*"

It felt good to give Lindy the freedom to see Lenn when she wanted and I was sure it would make our relationship that much stronger. It was funny too, but I felt less pressure on me after Lindy began seeing Lenn. Ever since she got back from South Dakota, she was much more the aggressor in our lovemaking then I was, and sometimes I worried that I may not have been satisfying her in the way I had in the past. It actually felt kind of comforting to know that if I didn't feel like doing it, I didn't have to feel guilty. She would get what she needed from Lenn. I wouldn't want anyone to hear me say it, but I'd always felt like Lindy wanted sex more often than I did. Since she'd been seeing Lenn, I didn't have to worry so much.

I went to a "Mind-Body" workshop at U.C. Davis with Will Schutz. Afterward I felt somehow transformed. There must have been 200 people all together in one big room. In one experience, we broke into groups of five. Three women and another man were in my group. We interacted non-verbally, moving our bodies to express feelings rather than using words. Later we talked about how we felt towards each person. I was amazed to find out that all four people liked me, particularly the women. Two of them said they were even turned on to me sexually. It was so nice to hear. I couldn't believe it at first, but they were very convincing with smiles and hugs. I'd never felt very attractive sexually to women. I thought women liked my intellect and quick wit and took the body along with it. In the nine years that Lindy and I had been together, I'd had lots of fantasies of women turning on to me but never had it happen before.

The next day at work I had a strong fantasy about making love to one of the secretaries. Terry walked in and smiled. I closed the door and we discussed the report she was working on. Slowly she got up and sat on my desk in front of me and we continued to talk as though nothing had happened.

33

She spread her legs wide so I could see the moisture beginning to show through her white panties. I slipped my fingers in along the elastic at her thigh. She moaned but continued talking about the report. I slipped her panties down her legs and ran my tongue around her moist lips. I unzipped my pants and stuck my cock up inside her. She started to gyrate and move her hips, faster and faster. I covered her mouth to stifle the scream when we both came. She stepped back off the desk, picked up her report, and left.

It didn't seem possible that we'd been married for seven years. I was 29 and Lindy 26. I picked up the rings and we went out to eat at a nice restaurant in Oakland. It felt great! It was like being on a new adventure. After all our talk about Open Marriage, we'd finally begun living it.

Lindy and Lenn hadn't been seeing much of each other, though Lindy seemed hurt that Lenn had been seeing other women and kept breaking dates with her. Lindy had been turning more to me and it was nice comforting and supporting her. I liked it. I felt needed again. It felt kind of strange hearing her talk about her relationship with Lenn. I felt more like a girlfriend than a husband, but she needed a friend and I was glad I could be there for her.

I finally went to see a doctor again about my physical problems. Everything had felt terrible for weeks. I had sprained my ankle three weeks before, and it was still hurting. My stomach hurt whenever I ate and I was having trouble breathing. The doctor thought I might have pneumonia, but that was crazy. "I don't have time to get sick. There's too much going on at work."

The sickness finally hit. I was in bed almost constantly for three weeks. I never knew pneumonia could knock the shit out of you like that. I didn't feel like doing anything, but Lindy was horney and wanted to make love and I wanted the closeness as well. I felt torn. I wanted to and I didn't want to. I ended up doing it, but I lost my erection a couple of times. Lindy ended up getting angry and I felt hurt and guilty. I felt bad saying "no" when Lindy wanted to make love. I didn't know what was wrong with my body, why it didn't work the way it was supposed to.

The whole episode with Lenn had the effect of building up a great deal of guilt and hostility in both of us that had never been expressed. Since I agreed to their having sex, I didn't feel I had a right to be angry or hurt. Yet, I had come running out, had broken my word to wait for Lindy, and so I felt guilty. I knew Lindy felt some guilt at having sex with Lenn since it caused me so much pain, but she also felt angry that I "couldn't handle it" after encouraging them to go ahead.

Although on the outside I appeared calm and I openly discussed our new experiences with sex, inside I was at war with myself. I believed in a new form of relationship based on trust and openness where we didn't try to bind another person to us and limit who they could be, but allowed them to be free. I felt strongly that Lindy's move towards "liberation" and equality was warranted, and that my feelings were worn-out remnants from the past that with work and commitment would come in line with my new philosophy. Yet the feelings were strong, the desires from the past were compelling. I still wanted a woman who would always "be there for me," to hear my feelings, dry my tears, send me back to the world of men where I would be respected as a healer of people's problems. She would bear the child, take care of him and the adopted one, so I could assume the distinction of being that rare breed of man who conquered the world, was praised and admired by his colleagues and loved and respected by his doting family because even though successful, he was a devoted husband and father. I wanted to live out my image of the "perfect man" and I wanted a woman to complete the picture.

If there was to be a battle I knew I wanted to be on the side of "right," on the side of progress. I wanted to be the new, liberated man of the future. I'd just have to whip my feelings into shape in order to do it.

Chapter Three

I Explore What I Am

"When A Woman Calls, You Must Go"

. . . Zorba the Greek

New Year's Eve always seemed to be a time when Lindy and I would talk about "other relationships." There was usually a party where all our friends attended, got drunk, and flirted with each other. Nothing usually happened, but it was exciting fantasizing about the wild evening.

I met Dena shortly before midnight. She and her husband had evidently done some experimenting and I told her a little about what Lindy and I had experienced the previous summer with Lenn. The retelling seemed much more fun than the actual experience, though the loving and sharing between friends seemed so positive and possible I still felt drawn to wanting to try it again.

I saw Dena a week later when I did some work at her house and I was just about floored when, after sharing a glass of wine, she made it very obvious that she'd like to make love. I was really taken aback. She told me she had really felt turned on at the New Year's Eve party and had come back after taking her husband, Bob, home and was disappointed to find I'd already left. There was so much going on inside me. I felt flattered that someone was really turned on to me, but I wasn't really very turned on to her. I enjoyed talking to her, but her body just didn't do that much for me. She seemed surprised when I told her that I had never made love to anyone other than Lindy. We'd talked a lot about it and I'd had lots of fantasies, but I'd never done it. "It was Lindy who had the affair last summer with Lenn." I felt a little foolish being honest about my lack of extra-marital experience. It reminded me of my first date in college with Lindy. She sounded so worldly and experienced; I implied, without really saying so, that I had had a number of lovers in the past. It was many months after we had been going together when we both finally admitted that our vast experience was limited to some heavy groping.

"How about just holding each other, that's not being sexual," Dena said with a shy smile. I didn't really feel comfortable doing that but it seemed innocent enough, and I had trouble saying "no" so I wrapped Dena up in my arms. I did start getting turned on when she started kissing me on the ear and I thought maybe we should just go ahead and make love. A part of me was saying, "You must be crazy holding back on an opportunity like this. You have a nice-looking, eager, turned-on female practically begging to be fucked and you quibble over a few details of comfort." We spent about two hours with me saying "no" and Dena saying "OK" and then both of us getting turned on with kisses, then me pulling back, cooling down and going back to just hugging. I felt like a junior high school girl holding off the aggressive and handsome football hero in the back seat of his Chevy. I finally went home, my virtue intact, with a promise to get together again.

The next night, I talked to Lindy about my experiences with Dena. She was very loving and supportive of me and my feelings. I expected her to be jealous, but she just seemed to be happy for me and encouraged me to pursue the relationship in any way that felt good to me. Again I felt torn. "Shit, here's a golden opportunity to have that affair you've been fantasizing for so long *and* your wife approves and supports you." Another voice kept saying, "But this is too easy, too good to be true. Something bad is going to happen, and besides now that the reality of having someone else is at hand, it doesn't seem quite that exciting."

I saw Dena a few more times socially and enjoyed her interest in me. I felt excited being in the position to decide if we "did it" or not.

The night I first talked to Lindy about Dena, I had a series of dreams. Usually I don't remember dreams but these were vivid. In the first I was walking alone in a strange city. A man picked me up and we began talking as we drove to my motel where he was going to drop me off. I indicated I was from out of town and wasn't doing anything for dinner that night. He suggested we eat together, but reconsidered when he remembered his wife was going to be there. He thought she might feel uncomfortable with a strange man. I suggested he have her get a friend and we'd make a foursome out of it, thinking that afterwards the girl and I could enjoy sex together. He decided that wouldn't work out and we dropped it. Later on, I had another dream that I was having an affair with someone. There was a knock at the door. When I opened it, I was suddenly facing a barrage of machine-gun bullets which peppered the whole room.

I woke up in a sweat, and, I had to admit that I felt somewhat ambivalent about all this "open marriage" kind of stuff. I wasn't sure that having an affair, even with Lindy's knowledge, was what I really wanted. I didn't really trust Lindy's support of my interest in other women. Part of me felt that she was trying to encourage me to have an affair in order to deal with her own guilt.

Two days later, Dena and I were at it again, touching and hugging, getting close and pulling back. That night I talked to Lindy about my feelings and ambivalence. Lindy seemed relieved that we hadn't been sexual. Dena and I played and hugged and we almost decided to go ahead and make love, but I chickened out at the last minute. I kept having the feeling of being used. "What does Dena really want from me? Is she just trying to fill the gap that her husband, Bob, has left?" Another voice, Zorba the Greek, kept saying, "When a woman calls, you must go." I felt like a yo-yo. It didn't make sense to me. I thought men were always ready to fuck, never confused, ready for new conquests. Now I was being pursued and I didn't know what to do.

I went for a long walk and let the confusion wash over me. Ever since I could remember I'd been the one pursuing girls and it was the girls who'd been saying "no." My fantasy was always to have a woman come after me, but now that it was happening I didn't seem to be able to handle it very well. I wanted to do what was right for me and Lindy and Dena, but I didn't know what it was.

Somewhere in the midst of the confusion I decided I didn't want to have sex with Dena and the most honest thing was just to tell her.

I went over to Dena's house with the kids on Saturday. It was nice — the kids played together and Dena and I talked about my feelings about us. I said I felt strongly that I didn't want to get involved sexually at this time but didn't want to let our friendship die. Dena seemed agreeable, though disappointed. We decided to have dinner together at our house — Dena, Lindy, me, and all our respective children. We all had fun. We drank and talked and felt like one big family. As it got closer to bed-time the level of tension seemed to go up. We decided that Dena would stay and spend the night. I said that I didn't want to sleep alone (I think I was afraid that they'd get it on, but didn't say that) or be sexual with either of them, and this seemed agreeable to all. We decided to all sleep together.

Three of us in bed was kind of fun, with me in the middle enjoying two naked females, and repeating to myself over and over, "You don't have to do anything you don't want to do." Mostly it felt nice, like three kids at a slumber party, with only a few flashes of fear — "if I roll over one way, she'll think I'm coming on to her and if I roll the other way she'll think I'm giving her the cold shoulder." All in all, it was just fine, until it got to be time to sleep for me. I'd found that I was one of a rather special breed of human beings who loves to snuggle, but when it's time for sleep I don't want anyone touching me. I couldn't imagine anything worse than rolling away from one body in order to get comfortable and rolling right into another one. It felt good and kind of freeing to announce that I was going to sleep in another bed alone. It wasn't easy but I was feeling stronger and more sure of myself, even if it didn't match the macho fantasy of "two tarts in a tub."

A few days later, Dena and I had our first sexual encounter. There was really no "decision," it just seemed to "happen" one night. I guess I got tired of being on the fence. I don't really know. Dena definitely seemed happy and I was too, though Lindy seemed threatened now that we'd actually begun being sexual. Why do feelings have to be so complicated?

Now That I've Done What I Should Do...
What Do I Want?

My work had always been a central theme in my life. Early on, I knew I wanted to work with people, something in the helping professions. Over the years, that dream had focused and for the last seven or eight years, I had spent a great deal of my energy reaching the top of my profession. I didn't think I'd moved ahead for the money, though that had been nice, or for the power, but just to move ahead.

I seemed to get bored with a job after about two years and wanted to do something new. I'd always found something else, a new step just waiting to be taken. But then I got confused. There didn't seem to be as many steps around to take. In the past, each step seemed obvious and easy. As soon as I had decided what I wanted to do next, usually someone offered me a job or a promotion within my present job.

For the first time in my life, everything looked bleak. I used to enjoy coming into work, usually arriving early so I could get started while things were still quiet before everyone poured in. But then I found myself feeling tired before I even arrived — and it got worse through the day. There was no clear direction for the "Continuing Care Project" I'd been working on for the last six months. There were no real supports in the system. Everyone was scared of losing their jobs and the creative energy was nil. Everyone acted like they were drowning and they each had an "every man for himself" attitude, enclosed in their own little cubicles and trying desperately to hold on. I needed some other options, some new answers to the question, "what do I want to do?"

Then my birthday came along, and it was an extra-special

one. I slept late, and had breakfast in bed while the kids were eating. Then I got up, with my eyes closed, and was given a surprise that I couldn't figure how Lindy could hide in the house — a new bicycle. I felt that age 30 was a real transition point for me. I wanted to exercise more, get more in touch with and comfortable with my physical being. It also felt like the beginning of more of an extended family for me. I never had much of a family growing up, just my mother. I'd always wanted more people around to interact with and share feelings with; I'd always wanted more adults for the children to get to know and interact with. We hadn't found the right people yet, but I was hopeful for the future.

I'd always been envious of people with large families. At holidays and family reunions, everyone seemed to be part of something larger than themselves. Everyone had a place. I'd never felt I really belonged to anything. Now though, I had the opportunity to create my own "extended family."

What I knew about communes wasn't really appealing. I knew nothing about farming and the thought of living in the country and growing my own food didn't appeal to me. Yet the thought of living with two or three other adults I liked and cared for, who shared work and responsibilities, definitely had possibilities.

Lindy seemed interested, though not as excited as I was about an "extended family." She grew up with a sister who dominated her and was not excited about repeating that process. Lindy and I had always had the view that was "me and you against the world." It felt nice to have someone special, someone I could count on for love and support. Lately, though, I was feeling restricted and wanted more room for us to grow. The thought of including other people in our family, extending our love to others, rather than holding it in closely, felt like a definite option for us in the future.

Open Marriage

New Year's Eve rolled around quickly again. Whoopee, a party over at Jim and Rita's. As we had done at the last New

42

Year's Eve party, Lindy and I had been talking about our fantasies of having an orgy or some other form of sexual adventure. It always seemed exciting to talk about — it was one of the areas of our lives where I really felt connected to Lindy. I also liked the feeling of finding new levels of consciousness, new ways of relating at our most basic levels of personal interaction.

New Year's Eve was great. Good friends, playing and dancing and flirting. Luann was there with her wet blanket, Joe. She had always been incredibly beautiful and sexy to me. I had always had an "ideal woman" fantasy when growing up, and she came pretty close to meeting it: a petite body, with long black hair, striking blue eyes, a tight, round little ass, slender legs, and a joy of living that radiated out of every pore. Well, we played around a bit and danced — until I felt Joe's eyes on my back. I tried to talk to Joe, but we didn't seem to have anything in common and I couldn't seem to make contact with him in any meaningful way. He had been a high school auto-shop teacher for years and all he seemed to know how to talk about were carburetors.

I danced with another friend, Rita, to old Jefferson Airplane albums and felt like I was back at the Fillmore in the 60's. Rita had style and grace. She was never pretty and no one would ever call her cute, but she was often beautiful. She loved the outdoors and mountain climbing and ran with the same dogged determination that she used to put herself through graduate school while raising two small kids. She often seemed cold and aloof to me, but also proud and free, like and Indian princess. I'd never danced with her before, though we'd been friends for some time, and it was a pleasant surprise.

By 4 a.m., everyone had left, except Lindy and me. We sat comfortably in front of the fireplace sipping wine and talking to Jim and Rita. It felt nice, like the family I always wanted and never had. Jim and Lindy sat close and touched gently and Rita moved closer to me and began rubbing my hand. We were all tired and a little drunk and quietly happy. There was some sexual energy bubbling quietly around, but no one had the energy to stir it or comment on it. We said goodnight and agreed to get together in a couple of days for dinner.

The same scene was repeated two more times over a period of a few weeks. The tension seemed to rise each time we all were together. Finally someone voiced what each of us had been thinking. "I'd like to be alone with her (or him)." It seemed fine and we all agreed. I took Rita home to my house and Lindy stayed with Jim. The children stayed in their own house and seemed amenable to having a new adult in the house when they woke up in the morning. The first time making love with Rita was exciting and somewhat tentative. What did she like? How did I tell her what I liked? What I most enjoyed was the sense of family, waking up in the morning with another person I cared about, getting up and playing music that Rita and I enjoyed and that Lindy never had liked. Just getting up early and dancing with someone who was a morning person like me, unlike Lindy, who would cringe at any sound before 10 a.m. It worked out great.

We called it the "basic 1-A switch." I went to Rita's or Rita came to our house and Lindy switched accordingly. No one was left alone. Everyone still had two children to deal with and two adults to deal with them. Now this was more like it!

The first anxious feelings came after a week, when Lindy wriggled up against me in bed, half awake and half asleep and moaned, "Oh, Jim." I rolled away and reminded her, "I'm Jed, remember." I felt hurt and angry, though I could easily understand getting confused in fantasy.

The easy balance of the basic 1-A lasted another two weeks. Lindy and Jim were entranced with each other and wanted to spend more and more time together. At first, Rita and I tried to keep up with their pace and felt something was wrong with us because we obviously weren't as passionate as they were. We finally said, "to hell with it." We didn't have to make love every time we stayed together, just because Jim and Lindy were probably fucking like rabbits. That took some of the pressure off and we enjoyed a number of friendly non-sexual evenings as well as the

44

opportunity to make love whenever we wanted.

It was obvious to both of us that there was little feeling of excitement or of being madly in love with each other. In fact, our relationship hadn't changed a great deal from what it had been in the past. We were friends who enjoyed socializing and spending some time together. Now we also occasionally made love. It was warm and tender and caring and not greatly different in intensity from dancing to old Jefferson Airplane albums.

Soon we dropped off being sexual and returned to being friends. Lindy and Jim continued their relationship, which seemed to deepen through time. We all wondered how the relationships would finally sift out.

I occasionally met other women and was sexual with them — whether out of competition with Lindy, loneliness, or desire for the women, I wasn't sure.

Lindy and I both seemed frightened of what the other person was going to do with others. We both wanted the freedom to see others, but didn't want to cause each other undue pain and wanted to keep our communication as open as possible. Neither one of us wanted to know the details of each other's sexual encounters and at the same time didn't want to be forever wondering whether the other one was screwing around anytime we weren't together.

We finally talked about our expectations of openness and agreed that each would take cognizance of the other's vulnerabilities and each would be responsible for what was communicated. We agreed that no specific details of sexual encounters would be shared, but that what *was* communicated would be honest. We both felt good about the talk.

Lindy and I decided to go on a cruise. We'd been spending so much energy with our "other" relationships we decided it would be nice to get away from the children and our other responsibilities and go on a cruise to Mexico. It was a fine set up: two professors were having a class on "human relationships" or some such topic, which meant it would be tax-deductible. We'd spend two or three mornings doing experiential exercises and the rest of the day and night we were free to play.

Lindy and I danced and ate and made love a lot. We laid out in the sun and visited Puerta Vallarta and other Mexican villages. I felt young again and we seemed to be capturing some of the innocence and excitement we had lost over the years.

There was a fair amount of sexual bantering going on among our little "class" and it felt good to have an "open" relationship where Lindy and I could talk about any attractions we felt. I was attracted to everyone, even a few of the men. I felt alive and free and potent and strong. Lindy said she was turned on to the young ship's officer who kept dropping by to say hello. We both agreed we weren't going to act on our sexual interest, which made the openness even better. We could flirt and play without worrying that things would go too far. I liked that feeling, free but not too free.

Alone in our cabin, I felt fat and happy. Lindy was still out with friends and I was enjoying the quiet of my own thoughts. I remembered the terror of our first sexual encounters, when Lindy would be out with someone and I'd be home alone torturing myself wondering what they were doing and whether she would ever come back. I felt more in control now, more able to handle Lindy being sexual with other men, though comforted to know she might be flirting but not sexual.

Lindy came in after midnight and without any preliminaries announced that she and the young mate had made love in his cabin. She said she hadn't intended to get involved sexually, but one thing led to another and .... I was furious. I felt betrayed and humiliated. "I'm here waiting for you and you're out fucking the crew." Lindy just listened. She didn't seem apologetic, which made me even angrier. After 20 minutes of yelling and pounding the bed, we crawled into our bunks for sleep. I felt once again that I'd been taken advantage of, been lied to. Much deeper, just barely conscious, was the envy that she'd scored and I hadn't, she could make "open marriage" work and I was a failure.

I have had a lot of gratitude for the feminist movement, feeling it has helped me be freer sexually. It was in reading feminist literature that I first found support in feeling that pleasuring myself through masturbation was good in and of itself, not just a poor excuse for pleasure when one didn't have a partner readily at hand. It made good sense to me, and if it was OK for a woman to get to know her own body, to find out what turned her on, then it had to be OK for me too. So much of my own growth in the past five years had come from women.

I remembered my first experience at masturbating. I was 10 or 11 and had spent the night with another boy in my class. We stayed up late and talked, and read comic books under the covers with flashlights so his parents wouldn't catch us. The summer night was warm and after talking about various girls in our class we liked, Ray told me if I rubbed my penis up and down real fast, it would feel good. Well, I tried it, and rubbed faster and faster, and although it got hard, I couldn't say it felt good. He assured me if I kept going it would get warm and sticky and feel good. I kept going, but after 10 minutes, I just felt sore and sweaty. If this was sex, I sure couldn't understand what the excitement was all about.

A few months later, I was playing with a massager my mother used to rub my stepfather's shoulders. I somehow began rubbing it over my cock and balls and it started feeling very good. The tension increased, greater and greater, until warm liquid shot over my legs and covered the machine. I was totally surprised and frightened, particularly when I looked down and touched my penis, which was strong and straight and full of life minutes ago and was now soft and dead. I felt very strange and the strangeness turned to fear and panic.

The only thing I could imagine was that I had somehow electrocuted myself. I remembered hearing about a kid who was killed when his radio fell into the bathtub.

"Oh God, please, I'm sorry. Please bring my cock back to life. I swear I'll never do it again."

It did return to life. But the truth is the next day I was back with the vibrator, and it was years before I learned I could get pleasure with my hand as well — and it was many more years later, after reading feminist literature, that I realized that others also knew about the pleasures of back massagers.

The Kid in the Candy Store

Well, it must be true that when you say you want something you create it in the universe, or as they used to say back home, "Be careful what you ask for, you might get it." Gloria was a lovely young woman that worked across the street at an insurance company. We just seemed to notice each other quite often, and it was a real turn on. She was young and fresh and beautiful and fun to talk with. She even sent me some terrible romantic poetry. The only problem was her husband — a highway patrolman who was very jealous and almost caught another co-worker and her in an embarrassing situation when he came home from the "office" unexpectedly during her lunch break. Since they carry guns at the office where he worked, I definitely decided to watch my step.

I found myself watching my steps walking close behind Gloria into her bedroom on our "lunch break," after she reassured me repeatedly that her husband never came home from work at this time. "What the hell, you only live once," I mused. Lunch hours became more and more interesting.

I began seeing Luann — my "ideal woman" — after a "human growth" workshop that I dutifully attended with my wife, who had just gotten interested in Transactional Analysis and insisted that I would learn a lot if I attended. She assured me a lot of our friends would be there. I hadn't seen Luann since the New Year's Eve party and was surprised that she was obviously interested in me. We flirted and touched and came pretty close to making love on the floor. Even though we were sure no one else had noticed our interest in each other, we decided to cool it for awhile.

Later that night, my stomach began hurting and my allergies and wheezing increased. I didn't understand why I seemed to have hurts and pains after I met new women. I really couldn't understand myself sometimes. In the morning, I thought a lot about Luann and also about Gloria. I felt like a kid in a candy store, who had just been given a $50 bill. I wanted it all. "One of those please, one of those, and no need to wrap that one up, I'll eat it on the way out." Let it all hang out! There was also a quiet but nagging little voice that I kept choking back that said, "This is wrong, the husband is going to get you." I also heard an even quieter voice, syrupy sweet, saying, "Come here, sweety, you're mine. Whatever Lola wants, Lola gets, and little man, little Lola wants *you*."

What did I want? Was I attracted to Gloria or Luann because I really wanted *them* or because they were available and seemed so drawn to me? With Gloria, I liked her sense of fun, her bubbly, free side, her sexual ease. But the hook with her was her pistol-packing papa. I'd been attracted to Luann ever since I first met her. She was my ideal of the beautiful woman I always wanted but never had the chance to touch because she was always on the arm of the captain of the football team. Now she was making it very clear she wanted me. I still couldn't really believe it. I mean, I was short and I had a big nose and was Jewish. I wasn't tall and never would be (even though my mother assured me, when I was 9 and 10 and 11 and 14, not to worry that I'd grow). I didn't look like Tony Curtis or Robert Redford, and I'd always known that women who look like Luann were not attracted to men who look like Jed. So what the hell was going on? Whatever it was, I decided I better jump on board, before I found out it was a dream and I had to wake up.

I did something I'd never done in my life, one of those things I used to see Jean-Paul Belmondo, or some such actor, do in the movies. I used to think, "Man I could do that, if I was only eight or nine inches taller, and was good-looking, and rich, and . . . ." Everyone from work went to have lunch together at the Bala Basque to say goodbye to someone who was leaving. The food was served family-style and it never seemed to end. We also got complimentary bottles of some kind of Basque wine that tasted terrible, but made everyone feel just fine. We laughed and talked and joked and bitched about work. When it was time to leave, we reluctantly got up and headed through the darkened restaurant toward the door. On the way out, I came up behind Lee, a beautiful young intern with hip-length black hair, large round breasts and deep mysterious eyes. With the wine and the family fun and the surreal quality of the inner sanctum of the Basque restaurant, I leaned toward her and whispered, "You know, what I'd really like to do is head somewhere else than back to work, find a secluded spot and make love to you." Just saying it made me feel six feet tall and as handsome as any swashbuckler that ever stepped off the screen, but I was still quite unprepared for her simple reply, "I'd like that too." We walked out together from the parking lot and decided in the bright light of day that we really had things we had to do back at work, but agreed to meet after work for a drink and discuss our mutually agreeable idea.

I spent the weekend with Lee in Sacramento and it was a total delight from the time I walked in the door and found her in a low-cut orange gown that showed off her brown body to perfection, until Sunday evening, when I felt exhausted. I felt more comfortable sexually with a new woman than I ever had before. What I liked most about her was that she was very specific about what she wanted without being demanding or feeling angry or hurt if I didn't want to do it. After playing and laughing for a long while, she turned, as easily as if she was asking for a cigarette, and said, "Would you go down between my legs and eat me?" I did it with pleasure, as much from her directness, ease, and excitement as from the physical pleasure of exploring her body.

God, where had these women been all my life? I couldn't seem to get enough.

I'd always had a fantasy of "making it" with the kind of woman who always seemed totally out of reach to me, but would someday take one look at me and fall hopelessly in love. Cassy was in a class I taught, and she seemed to match my fantasy exactly. She was very attractive and petite, with a yummy-looking body. She was my fantasied cheerleader, somewhat aloof, distant, the kind I always perceived would want a jock and never bat an eye at me. I spent at least an hour walking back and forth in my hot room thinking about calling her. When I finally called, after I had been dancing around drinking wine and feeling good, I was surprised by her warmth and enthusiastic acceptance of my invitation to get together. "You mean, right now?" "Yeah," I said sauvely, "right now." "Well, give me a half-hour to get dressed," she said.

I drove over feeling really good. I didn't really care what happened. I had actually stepped into my fantasy and talked to my dream, so anything that happened now would be just fine. When I arrived, I was again surprised at her warmth. We immediately sat down on the floor, opened up a bottle of wine and talked about marriage, divorce (she'd been divorced for four months), hassles with ex-spouses. It felt real and I was surprised. "Hey, people like that are just like me." It was kind of scary.

We sipped more wine, listened to more music, touched more intimately and talked more openly. I told her about my fantasy of making it with a cheerleader and she told me she had been a cheerleader in high school and in fact, had married a football hero, but after five years of marriage they didn't seem to do any better than the rest of us. I couldn't believe it, playing out my fantasy from a basis of honesty. It seemed like the merging of the sun and the moon, the best of everything. I felt transformed, part of another world. As the evening drew on and our talk was interrupted more and more with long kisses and hugs, the fantasy-honesty game was overtaken by sexual longing. We went into the bed-room and our lovemaking was like living on another dimension. A dream come true — all the girls who would never look twice at me because I wasn't tall and I wasn't a football hero and I didn't look like Burt Reynolds, all the movie stars I used to fantasize making love to, all wrapped up into one woman giving herself totally to me. I drove home in a cloud.

Porno Movies

Then an interesting incident occurred, when I finally got Lindy to go to another porno movie with me. During our 10 years together, we'd gone a couple of times, and though it stimulated lovemaking for both of us, Lindy always seemed reluctant to go. There was a new "adult movie" house in town, and it was reported to be more respectable than most. That meant that it was on the "miracle mile" and there were a minimum of drunks and broken bottles you had to step over to get to your chair. It *didn't* mean you could look around in the theatre to see if any of your friends were there.

Things went well through the first half of the movie. I enjoyed watching the action, hearing the moans and groans, and running my somewhat sweaty hand up Lindy's leg. The mistake I made was getting involved with the story line of the film, something I rarely had to guard against since there was rarely ever a story line in a porno movie. This one involved a guy who kept trying to get his wife to try their neighborhood swinging parties. He kept telling her how good it would be for their relationship, and she kept protesting that she wasn't interested in having sex with anyone but him. He finally convinced her to go, and though she was shy at first, she quickly caught on, and became the life of the parties. For awhile, they both enjoyed the swapping scene until he got tired of playing around and wanted to go back to their quiet, monogamous home life. She said, "No way. You introduced me to this excitement, and I'm not going back to being a dull housewife while all this is going on in the neighborhood," and off she went to meet the new black dude in town.

52

Well, all of a sudden, I wasn't turned on to the movie at all. I kept hearing "your woman wants some of that black stuff," and my stomach began to churn. What if it happened to me? What if Lindy started looking for some black guy with a 12-inch cock who was proficient in the Watts-Wanga stroke? She'd probably leave me. Goddam movie must have been written by a woman. They're supposed to make me feel potent and powerful, not anxious and insecure!

Learning to Say No

I ended things with Gloria. She had invited me to come over to her house on our lunch break and make love. I had felt uncomfortable, afraid her husband might come home unexpectedly and shoot me. She had reassured me over and over that he would never come home, so our liaison was set. The lovemaking was OK, definitely exciting, certainly more exciting because an element of danger was thrown in. What really got to me was that I found myself musing, "So what if he comes home, we've all got to die sometime. What better way to go than in the middle of an orgasm?" After I went back to work I realized that I was really taking a chance of getting killed and thinking philosophically about dying with my boots on (and pants down). That's great stuff for romantic folk songs and paperback novels, but anyone who really lives their life that way has got to be out of their mind. I realized the real undercurrent of self-destructiveness that's inherent in the macho game of "get the other guy's wife." She understood when I called to tell her I wanted to end things, and though she called a number of times afterward to invite me over "one last time," we kept the ending clean.

Ending the relationship with Dena wasn't as easy. Although we had both been seeing other people, there was something special about our relationship. She and her husband, Bob, had separated during the time we were together and Dena was drawn to me for support. Dena had been my first "extra-marital" sexual relationship and there was an innocence about it, like the first time I ever made love.

After rehearsing what I would say a hundred times, I went over and told her I wanted to end the relationship. She seemed stunned and kept asking me why. I didn't know why, but agreed there must be some logical reason. The more reasons I found, the more our conversation deteriorated. I felt I was drowning and had to get away to survive. I finally ended up walking out. The "no" was final, though, not clean, and it was years later before I was able to talk to Dena and tell her how much that "first time" meant to me.

Sex Without Women

I thought I knew now what women felt when they swore off men. I was tired of playing sexual games, getting myself up for some new adventure, and finding the reality much less enjoyable than the fantasy. The fantasy was simple, but the reality was complicated and cumbersome. I was never very good at relating sexually without getting involved with the person. When I was involved with them, I was also aware of their husbands and former lovers, children and friends, neighbors and co-workers. I also found that when I was sexual with someone else, I wanted to open up my emotions and heart to them and that didn't happen in a few weeks of passion. I wasn't that secure either, and when I was sexual I was very open and vulnerable. I didn't think I really felt comfortable trusting my feelings to someone I didn't know all that well. It helped in some way getting involved with friends. At least I could trust them, but once the friendship became a lover relationship, there didn't seem to be a way to go back to being friends once the sexual part was over. The whole thing was too complicated for me. I wasn't sure it was worth it.

I began doing some of the exercises in a book on sexuality I had gotten at the Center for Human Sexuality in San Francisco. The exercise on masturbation was interesting. The instruction was to concentrate attention on the sensations in my own body rather than fantasizing. At first, I found it difficult to get turned on at all without looking at pictures, or reading, or picturing some sexy scene in my mind. Gradually, I found the feelings pleasurable, but not highly stimulating, a kind of low plateau of sexual turn-on. I fantasized some scene and the turn on increased. I returned to just touching myself and focusing in on my physical sensations and the turn-on settled at a higher plateau. I eventually had an orgasm which was very nice and spread through my whole body. For the first time, I became aware that fantasies take me away from my own body. The orgasm is intense but over very quickly, and is very localized around my penis. When I concentrated more on the sensations in my own body, the pleasure seemed more total.

I liked the process of getting to know what felt good to my body, not just the stimulation of the fantasy in my mind.

What Good Are Men?

Lindy went away for the weekend with a friend from San Francisco. I spent the weekend learning to run with a runner named Mike Spino in Golden Gate Park. I felt so alive and part of the flow of the world. I experienced Saturday night alone, felt some loneliness, but also excited to be just with me. I met a man in a bar and we talked in an open, friendly way. I realized how few men friends I had in my life, how much had revolved around women. It was nice to just be friendly with a man in a bar, rather than seeing him as a potential competitor for some woman I had my eye on.

I used to envy women I would see in bars who were with a group of women friends. They looked like they were truly enjoying being together, not just waiting to meet a man. The men I'd seen had one hand on a bottle, one eye on the conversation they were having with the guy next to them, and the other eye and all of their attention on the women walking by.

It was a real treat for me to "forget" about women for awhile and talk to another man.

The following week I called up my friend Les and asked if he'd like to go out for a drink with me. It turned out to be a delightful evening. We talked about ourselves and our lives, our work, and our women. I realized I'd rarely ever spent an evening with a man, or any time for that matter, where we weren't *doing* something. I had known Les for several years and never knew he played the organ. Slightly drunk, I followed him into the darkened church where he played on Sunday. I sat in the pews while Les played some Bach selections in the dark. That truly was the most unusual Saturday night date I had ever had.

On Sunday, Lindy and I saw some friends, the Sorensons, and had a great afternoon talking. It was the first time that we had really talked to anyone else about what we'd been experiencing since we were no longer sexually monogamous. It was comforting to hear that David and Michelle had been open sexually for the past two years and were experiencing some of the same things we were. I was most surprised to hear David share his feelings about losing Michelle and his fears and insecurities about himself. I had always seen David as the strong, macho type. He ran 10 miles a day, raced bicycles in competition, and took people out for wilderness survival training. Yet there was David with a quaver in his voice telling Michelle he didn't like who she was going out with. And Michelle, who I'd always seen as the fearful, clinging type, was talking back with a strong voice and deep conviction, "I'm going to see whoever I damn well please." It still seemed strange, but at least there was one other person beside me who was having trouble with his wife's aggressive style in the world. It was nice to feel a kindred spirit.

Chapter Four

I Cannot Hide What I Am

Exploring the Dark Side

I need to go back in time for a bit, back to the 60's. In the fall of 1965, I had just dropped out of medical school and begun work at U.C. Berkeley in graduate school. Everything scared me. I was depressed most of the time and afraid I might do something foolish. I was afraid of being drafted and finding myself dead in Viet Nam. I was afraid of not doing something about Viet Nam for fear I would come to accept the killing as OK.

I had been reading my prescribed two hours of Viet Nam News a day and going to an anti-war rally each day in order to force myself to stay close to the things that terrified me the most. I thought if I didn't, I would just run away from everything. I felt I had run away from medical school and now I was afraid I would run away from Berkeley as well. Yet I was tired of going to the noon rallies and hearing again about what I should be doing to help the Vietnamese against creeping U.S. aggression. Instead of going to the rally one day, I decided to go hear about an organization called Synanon, some kind of drug treatment center that had opened up in San Francisco.

The Synanon speakers surprised me. Instead of talking about the drug problem in the abstract, they talked about their own lives, the ways in which they had tried to hide from themselves, to be something they weren't. They said they found in Synanon a place to begin to grow up, to stop running, and to begin to find out who they were under the surface images they had developed. One was a Puerto Rican from a ghetto in New York, another a black from

Oakland, and the third was an educated Jew from Los Angeles. They all were quite different, yet shared a similar path. They didn't "fit" with the American ideal when growing up, and they had all turned to drugs to escape their pain and find an identity that was their own. They had all bounced around mental institutions and prisons trying to be cured, and they had all found Synanon and were now learning to live. They explained the basis of the Synanon philosophy, taken from Ralph Waldo Emerson, "The unexamined life is not worth living." They had come together to help each other learn the lessons that schools couldn't teach. There were no therapists in Synanon and no patients, only people learning to get beyond their anger and judgments, their prejudice and denial.

I was fascinated. Although I had never so much as smoked marijuana and could count the times I had been drunk on three fingers, I felt drawn to the Synanon people. When they announced that they were planning to start a Synanon group on campus, I signed up immediately.

With all the social protest of the huge, impersonal university and the Viet Nam war, people in Synanon were saying, "You've got to change yourself first" — and somehow comparing the self-assured, excited, open faces of the Synanon "Game players" with the dour, fearful faces of my professors in graduate school, I was beginning to believe them.

I found the Synanon Game to be a place to examine in depth who I was, to connect my ideas to my emotions, to learn how to "feel" the feelings I had been taught never to express.

I remember Chuck Dederich, Synanon's founder, saying to some newcomer, "Lad, go find yourself!" and when the newcomer said, "Oh, thanks Great Wise One," Chuck went on to say, "What in the name of God does it mean George, go find yourself!" I asked myself the same question. When I graduated from junior high, my mother wrote in my year book, "This above all else to thine own self be true and it must follow as the night, the day, thou cannot then be false to any man." I knew immediately that it was true and that I should lead my life in a way consistent with my beliefs, and I'd been working hard on that kind of life all these years. But I realized, hearing Chuck Dederich, that I didn't have any idea what "to thine own self be true" meant, and I didn't know how to go about finding that true self.

Something Chuck was saying struck a very deep chord in me. "In Synanon, an opportunity is provided to open the door. It's a key to the room where you are; the room that life has locked you into where you can't find yourself. You stand inside that door, inside that room (you don't even know where the door is), and there you are . . . in there. You can't find yourself. But, there is a key. We know that if one takes this key in his hot little hand and inserts it into the lock and twists hard enough, that door will open. The door will open a little at a time and you'll begin to find yourself." Well, I wanted some of that knowledge that my mother didn't seem to be able to give me, and that my 18 odd years of school didn't seem to be able to give me. I was open to giving Synanon a try.

During the next six months, I thought I'd made a mistake. In their Games, all I could see were 10 people sitting in a circle in an old warehouse in San Francisco called the Sea-wall, yelling and screaming at each other. When it was my turn to be on the "hot seat," I'd get something like, "Hey dummy, why don't you get off some of that shit you've been sitting on all your life . . . or "fuckin" intellectuals — all you know about life is what you read in books. Why don't you tell us who you really are behind all that head-tripping you do all the time." After two and a-half hours or so, the groups would end and 200 or so people would sit around having coffee, laughing and joking about how great the "Synanon Game" had been. I thought they were all crazy, yet there was something interesting about all the excitement generated each week when we'd come over for the "Game."

I would sit quietly each week trying to understand what everyone was yelling about, asking a few questions when I could get a word in, and making what I thought were acute psychological statements when it looked like someone was getting too much dumped on them. That's when the group would usually turn on me. "What the fuck's the matter with you, asshole? What makes you think she is so weak she needs you to defend her? Let's talk about *your* scared little ego that's terrified that someone is going to find out who you really are." I would calmly answer that I didn't know what they were talking about. I wasn't hiding anything or defending anything.

For weeks afterwards, I went home after the Game wishing I could tell those mother-fuckers a thing or two, wishing I could yell back and tell them to go fuck themselves. But I wasn't angry and I never used language like that, and my pride told me that letting them get to me, or showing them my feelings, was weakness. One day in the Game, someone said something that triggered rage in me. Before I could turn it off or censor it out, there came a barrage of anger. Fucks and mother-fuckers flowed like wine from a broken bottle. All the anger and rage that "I never had" came out, feelings from my childhood, growing up, Viet Nam. When I was finished, I couldn't believe all that had come out of me, yet I felt light and free, I felt proud of the smile I got from one of the old-timers. "Not bad, professor, I think there may be hope for you yet."

I spent five years involved with Synanon, allowing myself to feel more and more, to express what I felt without trying to be nice or tactful or appropriate. For three hours a week, I found I could practice being myself. The rest of the time, I could decide whether I wanted to be honest or discreet. At least I was beginning to learn the difference, and was beginning to learn what it meant "above all else to thine own self be true...."

The letter I wrote to the Director when I left Synanon summed up my feelings.

"I grew up during the time I was at Synanon. I learned a little bit about myself and some about people. I got married the first summer I was at Synanon and brought my wife into the Game Club. I learned what it meant to be a man and what being a husband was all about.

"I'm leaving Synanon, though, and it feels good and

right. Maybe because I know I'm not really leaving, that Synanon is inside me and a part of me. But in another sense, I am leaving and that is very real. I'm afraid of the unknown, of what life will be like without Synanon, if my marriage will be as strong and beautiful without the game and the environment, and how I'll relate now with the friends I've made in Synanon. I'm also afraid of the world out here, afraid of the violence and self-destruction this country is engaged in. I'm afraid of the increasing polarization in this society, afraid I'll end up in the middle and get murdered by both sides.

"Much of the turmoil that Synanon has experienced in the past year and continues to experience is due in part to the growth pains of the community and the pains of the members as they 'snap' to the fact that they are no longer patients and must choose their own future. Many run in terror at the reality of their own freedom and the necessity of making a choice, and there really is little difference between the terror of a Synanon member who came in as a 'dope fiend' or one who came in, like me, as a 'square'.

"I'd like to thank Synanon, the people, and the community for all I've gotten and I'd like to thank a couple of individuals that I have some special feelings for. I want to thank you for the experience of my Trip, I'd like to thank Miriam for demonstrating how to ask for friends, John Maher for trusting and caring about me, Chuck for teaching me what 'Lad go find yourself' means, and Margo Peterson for the courage to do it."

After Synanon, everything took on a different flavor. Feelings from the past that I had forgotten began to surface. I remembered my pain and confusion when I was four and my father was taken away one evening. My mother told me he was "sick" and had to go to a hospital. He didn't look sick and I didn't understand when she tried to explain that he had an "emotional breakdown" and went to a "mental hospital." I remembered the night I was five and my mother had left me briefly at night while she took a friend home. As it got darker, I began to panic and was in the front crying hysterically when she arrived. I was sure she was never coming back. I remembered my stepdad's involvement with us, the many times he came and left. As soon as I felt some love and showed it, he would disappear. I learned that it was safer to keep my feelings inside. I thought I had gotten used to his leaving and when he left for the last time when I was 13, I thought it didn't hurt much at all.

In Synanon, I had learned that the pain doesn't go away, it just gets buried deeper and eats away slowly from inside. Each painful memory, each experience of the dark side of my being, the side I had always hidden, allowed the pain to surface and the healing to begin.

Let Her Be Free, But Not That Free

With Lindy, I began gradually allowing my real feelings to surface and stopped being the "nice" guy that my fear told me I had to be in order to keep her. She was out late with one of her male friends. After pacing around trying to concentrate on TV, I finished the rest of a cake. Well, let's be honest. I finished the rest of the cake at 10 o'clock that I'd started eating at 9:30. By the time she got home, I was jealous and angry and I wasn't about to push it down inside as I had so many times. "I'm tired of being the dutiful husband that waits at home while you're out screwing around. It pisses me off when we make love and I see bruises left by some other man. It turns my stomach and makes me want to puke. Where are the fucking priorities?" Lindy listened and said she could understand my anger and discomfort, but had to continue to be honest with herself and seeing other men was important to her.

I had to admit, if only to myself, that a big element of my and jealousy was envy. "How come she's doing so well with her life, making new friends, drawing men to her like crazy? All I can seem to do is struggle. I feel like Lindy is moving past me and I don't know how to stay up with her and I'm afraid to tell her." I also had to admit that I was feeling more and more dependent on Lindy. I had grown up knowing that it was women who were dependent on men, that it was the women who begged the men not to leave as they clung with tears in their eyes. Now it seemed turned upside down and I didn't understand it. Yet, all around me I saw the same thing. Women were dependent on men financially and men were dependent on women emotionally, and it was the women who were taking the lead in overcoming their dependent status. We men just seemed to be slowly shriveling inside, while we beat our chest proclaiming how independent we were.

I felt torn. On the one hand, I felt Lindy had a right to be free to develop her own talents, to have fun, to be with others. But then she seemed to go all out, become wild, go "native." Why couldn't she be free with a little more restraint?

Confronting the End of the Dream

I remember one particular Sunday which was smooth and peaceful. I talked with Mom, played in the park, talked to my friend Dale. I felt much at peace with myself. Somehow the weight of the previous four years, since Lindy's trip to South Dakota, had been lifted. I was really glad to hear from Lindy when she called after her weekend away. I wanted to hurry and get her, but didn't feel panicky at the thought of waiting. I could finally contemplate life without her as an option.

I had a dream the next night. Lindy was coming home with a man from her weekend at Yosemite. Both of them were covered with dirt, as though they had been making love on the ground. They seemed indifferent to my concerns and I was angry and said, "If you want to get it on, that's fine with me, but I'm leaving." It was a realistic dream of my feelings.

We finally had our talk, and it felt good. I was straight and pretty clear and I thought Lindy heard me. I said I didn't want to continue to be angry and resentful when she was with other men and I was tired of living with the continual tension and anxiety I had felt.

It was clear that she needed the freedom to relate sexually

to other men, and I made it clear that I felt it was no "sickness" for me to feel jealous and angry. Her response was that she could handle my jealous and angry feelings as long as I didn't withhold sex as a way of getting back at her. We seemed less far apart on our sexual concerns than I thought. She wanted me to direct the pace in our sexual relating and take responsibility for both of us being satisfied, and I would have been happy to do that if I felt better about my ability to satisfy her. She also said she didn't want to play the role of always being there to put Jed back together. I could understand her feelings, but also had to say that I needed more nurturing from her and needed to feel special and unique.

We discussed openly the possibility that it might not work out for us and that we would choose to split up if it didn't. We also talked about what it would mean for each of us and for the kids. I felt a lot of fear had finally gone from me. We made love that night and it lasted longer, and had more play, than in the past, though it was still pretty constricted. Lindy didn't have an orgasm, but we stayed close and fell asleep together.

It had been a real struggle for me just to keep going. My two main sources of support in my life — my work and my wife — had all of a sudden not been there for me. In the past, whenever one was not going well, I had the other one to fall back on. Neither was there now. I felt lost, though very glad that I had Les and Frank and some of my men friends for support. I think unconsciously I'd been developing my male friendships over the past year "knowing" Lindy and I might split.

Lindy and I talked again, late at night. I told her again that I wanted more nurturing than I was getting. I'd been very down for a month, since I realized that after working for seven years in the mental health system, I no longer felt we really helped people at all. It had been like the death of a lifelong dream. I had been so sure the dream would happen. I would work my way up in the system until I could make some real change. I just needed time. But now the dream was dead and it was as if a part of me had died too.

My old pattern had been to break down and have Lindy give me the support to go back out and fight again. But I was reluctant to play the role we'd been through so often in the past. I was tired of breaking down at home, being glued together, and going back out to fight the next day. Lindy was also tired of playing Florence Nightingale. It was like we were in a play and couldn't use our old accustomed lines. We seemed to fumble around trying to "get something going," trying desperately to connect with each other. After being together for 12 years, we felt like strangers who thought they knew each other but couldn't remember having met.

At times, the discomfort turned into fear and then panic. If after 12 years together, I was living with a stranger, life didn't make sense. My previous ideas about what it might be like if we ever split up weren't anything like this. It never included that feeling of deadness that kept gnawing at my insides.

I tried to understand the difference between Lindy and my mom. I didn't need Lindy's love in the same way I needed my mother's love. I needed to remind myself that I wasn't a dependent little two-year-old child, even though I still had that part inside me. I needed to accept the reality that I wouldn't die if Lindy and I split up, and that I could make it on my own without her.

Lindy and I talked and there was some real caring between us. We identified some of the continuing blocks for us sexually. We were able to acknowledge that we each wanted someone different than we had. I wanted someone more caring and nurturing. She wanted someone stronger and less emotional. We had both become increasingly aware that demanding that the other person give us what we wanted just drove them farther and farther away.

Then came our monthly anniversary, something we always remembered together, number 108 or something like that, and I got angry about Jim coming over and calling. Lindy returned my anger, saying I was trying to control her. She argued that it was her house too, and her friends and she should be free to enjoy herself. I could hear her point and she was able to hear my feelings.

It felt increasingly good to express my feelings, though I was surprised I was still so jealous.

We talked about our own sexual involvement with each other and agreed that each would be more active in getting pleasure. I wouldn't be so preoccupied with doing it right, and Lindy wouldn't be so concerned about holding herself back for fear of upsetting me. We had nice, free, easy sex that night.

But sexual life continued to be a source of tension between us, even though we kept trying to improve things. The more I tried to go more slowly (at Lindy's request), the more I felt mechanical and rejected (she probably didn't ask Jim to go slower and slower and *slower.*) We finally stopped and talked. "Fuck, you want me to do the right things to bring you to orgasm, but you don't tell me what to do. The more I try, the more you reject. Give me some feedback. Let me know what you want." Lindy replied, "I've told you before what I want. You just don't care about me, or want to satisfy me. If you did, I wouldn't have to give you step-by-step instructions."

"I feel assaulted," Lindy said. I screamed back, "I'm not assaulting you, damn it!"

Both of us had settled for getting "fucked," but felt hurt and resentful at the lack of intimacy, trust, caring, and playfulness we used to have. I realized I'd been kidding myself in hoping that she really wanted to make love, hoping somehow if we could just "get started" the good feelings would begin to come back.

I began to realize that things had been bad for so long I had come to expect "disaster" every time we made love, and though part of me was there in our lovemaking, most of me wanted to get it over with as soon as possible since I knew it would end in failure anyway. Though I could see that my feelings were just making things worse, I couldn't seem to do anything to change things.

Lindy and I had dinner at one of our favorite restaurants. It felt like it had been a long time since we did anything just for fun without worrying about what we'd get into this time. After a few glasses of wine, we began talking about our "love affairs." It was a nice sharing, reflecting on the people in our lives we had loved and who had loved us. As we talked, I realized that my most important love affair had not been with any of the women we had been talking about but with my "work." As I talked about "her," work became like another person and I got tears in my eyes realizing how important she had been for me. My career had been my true love, at times a wife, at times a mistress. So much of my dream to be someone had been wrapped up with her.

But my job at the mental health center was coming to an end, and so too was that part of my career. I wasn't moving on to something else and I felt like someone very close to me was on the verge of death. Even though I had come to hate her, had fought and struggled with her, I loved her still and always would. Lindy sat across from me crying for the men she had lost. I cried for my career, and we both cried knowing how far apart we really were.

Macho Revisited

In my loneliness, I sought comfort with my friend Larry's sister, Lisa. She was visiting from Wisconsin, and since Larry was busy with work, I volunteered to show her the sights of the City. After a day together, it was obvious that Lisa was entranced with me. She sat for hours and listened to me talk about myself. She was there when I wanted to interact but left me alone when I had something else to do. I loved it all, but it also scared me.

Maybe I had been kidding myself in thinking I wanted a liberated, self-assured "whole" woman. Maybe I was really like Joe, my stodgy teacher friend, and really wanted a passive, well-dressed, made-up female to sit at my feet and bring me my slippers at night. Shit, that would really blow my image. How the hell could I continue to teach classes on "Alternative Lifestyles" and lecture about the joys of being a "liberated new-age husband" if what I really wanted was an old traditional marriage? And worse yet, I would have to admit that Lindy was right, and if I really allowed myself to think about wanting that kind of relationship, I would have to acknowledge that our marriage was over.

I'd spent my life trying to find out, then live out, my image of a "good man." Now when I thought I at least knew what I was looking for, I found out what I really wanted was what I'd been rejecting all these years. Could I really let go of my image as a liberated man and move back three steps and be just like all the other macho woman-haters I despised? I sure as hell didn't like the image, but I'd been unhappy so long with a "fine" image, I thought I'd rather be happy for awhile and have a "fucked" image.

Maybe I Am as Bad as I Feared

"The camper for us is the parenting van," I screamed at Lindy, "for you and Jim, it's the traveling motel." I felt like I was just the bad filling sandwiched between times of fun with Jim. "I don't like any of the changes that are going on in your life. I know it was my idea to 'open' the marriage, but I don't like you sleeping with other men and I don't like you getting so independent. I don't like being with the children and sometimes I'm not even sure I like the children all that well. Damn it, I want you home where you used to be." I stormed off to be alone.

I read something by Betty Dodson and I became aware that my fear of losing Lindy had controlled me all along. Once I let that down a little, I was overcome with a lot of stuff I'd been pushing down because I wanted to keep Lindy and I wanted to keep my image of a liberated man.

As Dodson pointed out, and I had to agree from my personal experience that even us liberated, liberal men were not ready for the real changes in females. No matter what overlay of liberal philosophy I'd gained over the last 10 years, I still was raised on the myth of the passive woman who waited for her man, who supported him in times of need, who was always there when he needed her, who experimented with sex only within the limits that he prescribed, who was ultimately sexually monogamous and would enjoy sex with him more than sex with others, even if it was lousy, and who believed that a woman's place was in the home with the children. And that's the way it had been with Lindy and me the first seven years of our marriage.

In reading *A Man's Guide to Women's Liberation*, I realized that I was scared of Lindy. I was confused and angry and aware that I was having difficulty relating to a real, grown woman. I really did have a problem with my sexuality, with my feelings about myself as a man and Lindy as a woman. I'd been hiding behind my books and my liberal philosophy, but I was as scared as Joe, always hovering over Luann. It was no accident that Lindy, Dena, and Rita in some way threatened me sexually. All three were real, growing, active women who knew what they wanted, and I felt frightened and confused.

It was difficult to admit that regardless of other problems we all had, this was a big one and it was mine alone. I wished I could get a trade-off from Lindy in some way, so I could feel we were *both* working on things, but the main reality of our situation had to do with how I saw Lindy and her changing role, and that was totally my problem. I knew I wanted to do something about it, and I was scared. I realized, too, that I was tired of trying to be something I wasn't — liberal, liberated, understanding, together, etc. "Fuck all that shit."

Sexist Pig

To be honest, I'd say that I felt, when all was said and done, I could take care of myself. I was not the sniveling rag that I often acted like when I felt under pressure from Lindy. I am a chauvinist male! I had thoughts like, "Outside sex for Lindy feels wrong to me. If she does it, she's a whore. Her main responsibility is with the kids. Mine is to earn a living for the family. Her making a real income would threaten me. I don't mind her doing woodworking as a hobby, but what if she became a successful artist? I want her to be passive but responsive in bed and make me feel like a

69

man. I expect her to be there when I need her, to nurture my hurts. I must succeed and be perfect as a breadwinner, as an innovator and trailblazer, as a father, lover, husband, man, person, always at the forefront." I had been trying to live up to my image of myself at all costs. I'd become very dependent on Lindy for giving me courage to follow my job instincts, for validation in the way I looked, the way I cut my hair and the clothes I wore, for validation that I was good sexually, for keeping a home and family I could be proud of and come home to, and for intimacy.

When having sex with women, I expected myself to know it all and resented being told what to do or how to do it. It made me feel stupid. I felt most of the time when with a woman that I had to please her. I had a great fear of failure. No matter how much she said she enjoyed me, I didn't quite believe she was telling the truth. No matter how satisfied she seemed, I feared she would always want something more, something I couldn't give — and then she would leave me when I couldn't do it. I had a funny mixture of beliefs that women should be passive and frail and that women were strong and powerful and men must serve them.

I spent some time alone beside a stream in the mountains. Thoughts and feelings seemed to bubble up and flow over me. I realized how out of touch I had been with my own needs and wants since I'd been operating from so much fear in the sexual arena and, therefore I had been giving Lindy unclear messages about what I wanted:

For her to be more active sexually — no, that scared me.

To give me feedback about what she wanted — no, I felt like a fool.

To have an orgy — no, that scared me a lot.

To have group sex — no, I'd somehow be left out of the group.

To exchange with another couple — no, I wasn't that interested in sex to put up with the complications of multiple relationships.

To tell me her problems — no, if she was weak, who

would take care of me?

Looking back on my fantasy fling with my cheerleader, I realized there was more to my feelings than the joy of living out my adolescent dreams of conquest.

I realized there was still a lot of hostility in me from being a guy the beauties never gave a second glance. I remembered vividly being at a party in high school and asking one of the beauties to dance with me and getting a look of disdain and a curt, "No thank you." I remembered in dance class the number of times I was turned down by the beauties and quickly learning what "types" were available to me. I remembered the anguish of sitting on one side of the hall with the other boys while the teacher announced a "girl's choice" dance, and waiting as one after another boy was chosen while I sat and waited.

So, my cheerleader Cassy seemed to embody for me the living out of the "light" part of the fantasy. "Beauty falls in love with the beast . . . she fucks like crazy and they live happily ever after." I also began realizing the "dark" side of the fantasy. "Beauty falls in love and is swept off her feet, and as she lies panting, begging to be loved, I say, 'fuck yourself, bitch. You never gave a shit about me all those years when I needed a beauty to love me. Well, it's too late now'." It surprised me to realize how much hate I still felt towards women.

A Tiger at Work /A Wimp at Home

Over the past year, it had begun to feel as though I were leading two lives. At work, I was sure of myself, articulate, and strong. I was respected by both the men and women as extremely competent at my job and particularly adept at interpersonal realtionships. I was forever helping other people solve their problems and I seemed to know exactly what was needed in any situation.

When I would drive home I'd feel the energy seep out of me. I could almost see it in a long stream along the highway. As I drove up to the house I felt empty and drained. For awhile, I could still act strong. I remembered what it felt like and I could turn it on when I came into the house. The kids still responded quickly to my demands and Lindy and I fought a lot. I usually won the battles and felt badly that Lindy was hurt but thanked God I could still fight and nobody seemed to know I had lost my stuff. But gradually, that changed. I couldn't consistently pull it off. I'd win some and I'd lose some and I could see it in their eyes. They knew I was faking it.

In the mornings I would get dressed and then when I drove to work, my energy and power seemed to fill back up. I never could figure out where it came from, but I was glad it was there. I'd walk into the office and I was my same old self, independent, assured, confident. My being at home seemed like a bad dream. I knew that person wasn't really me, that I could be powerful if I really wanted, but there was no honor in fighting a weaker opponent. Besides, work was where it was important to show your stuff, that's where it mattered if I was strong, and I was doing fine there. In fact, the worse the dream got at home the better I seemed to do at work. I was taking on more and more responsibility, working longer hours, and producing more and more.

I began to dread coming home and tried to get it over with as quickly as possible. I grabbed the paper as soon as I got in the door, talked briefly with the children, then tried to lose myself in the news of someone else's tragedies. Lindy wanted to talk, but I was tired. I just wanted some peace and quiet. I stopped yelling, we stopped arguing, and things went more smoothly for a while. Something to drink became a staple of the evening ritual. Lindy seemed to alternate between angry withdrawal and angry confrontation. I just got more and more quiet.

The worst part was being in bed together. It hurt to remember the spontaneity and the warmth, the giggles and fun we used to have. I wanted it again, but was afraid if I opened myself up, if I let Lindy know how empty I felt, I would lose the little I had left. Trying to just save something, anything at all, became what I lived for. And I watched myself lose the little I had, drop by painful drop.

Chapter Five

I Am Just Fine As I Am

I Don't Want to Be Fixed

Once I opened up the "dark side" of myself and confronted the parts of me that had seemed too scary to even acknowledge, I felt free for the first time in years. I could begin to look at Lindy and me without filtering what I saw through the lenses of my fears of "abandonment" I had built up over the years.

I began seeing that the issue with Lindy related to my feelings of being scared and getting turned off by her aggressiveness and sexuality, her desire to have more control in the sexual relationship. It translated into feelings that she wanted things I couldn't deliver and would therefore leave me.

The other issue was one of strength. She said, "Be strong;" she was tired of playing Momma and nursing my insecurities. My fear was that she really wanted a man who was emotionally strong all the time, and she didn't want *me*, she wanted some image of what she thought I was. I wanted to find my strength again, but couldn't seem to do it while Lindy continued to be sexual outside our marriage.

Little by little, I was beginning to release the image I had of myself that demanded that I be able to handle anything, including my wife being sexual with others. In the past a man of strength would knock her around if she even thought of being disloyal. The new man of strength, I believed, would learn to conquer his anger, subdue his jealousy, control his confusion and fear.

To fail at this was to acknowledge that deep within I was a monster living only for myself. The new dragon to slay was

73

this beast within. Yet another voice was beginning to say, "What's wrong with being weak?... what's wrong with saying I want a woman who is sexual with me only?"

Lindy wanted us to go to a sex therapist. If we could just get that part of our relationship fixed up, she was sure everything else would fall into place. It was a very strange experience for me. We tried to pick someone who was "enlightened" and could understand all our open relationship issues without judging one of us as being bad or wrong. The last time we had seen a therapist, the man seemed to have a subtle bias towards men and had a difficult time relating to Lindy, particularly her outside sexual activity. We picked a woman this time, hoping to find someone more objective. Lindy thought she was great. She praised Lindy for her courage in following her own instincts and developing her sexuality in a way that was right for her.

This time the little voice in me was getting stronger. "What about me, what about my feelings, what about my sexuality? Is this the price I have to pay for living in a society biased in its advice on behalf of men?Now I'm expected to say 'OK, now it's your turn to walk on *my* head, to hell with the way I feel, if it works for you it must be right.' Well fuck that shit. There's got to be a better way than going through life trading off who will play the role of victim to your mate's oppressor. I'm getting tired of looking deeper and deeper inside to find the problem that I've got to get fixed. *I'm tired of being fixed.*"

It happened rather quickly. We had spent the holiday in the park picnicking and playing with the kids. We should have been happy. There were so many weekends in the park when we were. But now I felt dead inside and very, very sad. That night was even worse.

I realized that I couldn't take being together that night, getting in the same bed yet feeling a million miles away. I couldn't stand to cry again inside while we rolled over to our separate sides of the bed. There was so little to say. I wanted to scream out my love, my hurt, my rage, but there was no room now to do that, so I decided to leave. It felt right to take care of myself, to honor that voice inside that said, "You've got to please yourself first." It had been so long since I'd acted on that statement which I supported so strongly in others but had had such a difficult time carrying out in my own life. I'd been trying to please some other person, some other image, but not me. I was beginning to feel my needs strongly, and this time I decided to go with my feelings. Then the fear began to creep up around me like a choking fog. This might mean the end. I'd never be with Lindy again. I missed my children already, and kissed them as I left. I wished them well. It felt at first like a superficial "just saying goodnight gesture," but I knew it meant a great deal more. The tears stung my cheeks as I walked out of the room.

I knew I couldn't live with Lindy for long without love. It hurt too fucking much. My anger would come out at the kids, particularly Gene. He was confused, and didn't understand why I yelled. I didn't want to feel the hurt anymore that made me lash out at him. I remembered a song from the past, "Isn't it a long way down and isn't it a strange way down?" Not so strange. All our friends were down. No one seemed happy anymore, but I never thought it would happen to us.

I spent the night with a friend, and it helped clear things up for me. I couldn't even say what changed, but leaving the house that night had been an act of love to myself. When I returned the next day, Lindy seemed relieved that one of us had finally done something.

When Lindy said, "I want to sleep in separate beds," I immediately responded, "OK that sounds right to me," and I felt it. I wasn't ready to say it was all over and proclaim my singlehood, give up on the marriage, but I was tired of trying to change *me* to save the marriage. I realized that if I did that there wouldn't be any of me left to give to a marriage. I wanted to be me and feel OK about that, to deal with my sexual barriers at my own pace, not on a time ultimatum, even if it meant we split permanently.

I was aware that I scared myself with words like "disaster," and "all alone," when I talked about splitting up. But when I considered the reality of it, it wasn't so scary. A lot of the fear came from "failing just like my father did. He couldn't handle the responsibilities of marriage and a family and finally ended up in a mental hospital, and if we split up that's what I have to look forward to." I realized I didn't have to play out that drama.

Over the next week, I moved myself upstairs and made a little nest for myself in my office. Some of the tension had finally eased and I was beginning to get the sense that whatever happened in the future, we had at least stopped hurting each other. I was beginning to feel the first lightness inside I could remember in a long, long time.

The following week, Lindy and I agreed that I would move out of the house. I found a converted garage at a friend's house and though it was musty, it felt like a home.

I moved out of the house on a Tuesday into the spare room at Dale and Jan's place. It was really nice. Gene helped me move one day, and Sandy helped me the next. Gene seemed to be taking the separation just fine. Sandy, two-and-a-half years younger, was obviously insecure and clung tightly to me, asking over and over again when I was coming back. God, it took a lot of trust in my decision to stick with it when she cried and said, "Daddy, I don't want you to go." Lindy and I made arrangements and agreements about what I would do around the house as part of my "continuing family responsibilities."

I made the move and it felt right. Looking back over our 12 years together, I realized she had become at first my best friend, then my only friend, and eventually we smothered each other. When she began to grow and stretch out on her own, my fear alternately gave her support to do things I thought I could "handle," then pulled her back with my resentment of her freedom.

Two weeks after we split up, things felt fine. It wasn't nearly as bad as I had thought it would be. I found several nice women to spend some evenings with, and most of the evenings ended with us in bed. The sex wasn't spectacular, but it was pleasant, and it let me know I was still attractive to women.

I realized when I came to babysit the kids that it was Lindy's house, and I felt the first pang that "she's having a man over when I'm gone." I told myself that what she did with her time was her own business, but it hurt that I seemed to be so easily replaced. The dates I had had seemed different somehow.

The "honeymoon" period of the separation lasted about a month. It felt like I was moving through the stages of grief. At first, I was surprised that I didn't feel much hurt or pain, just relief at being finished with all the hassles of our interaction over the past few years. Even the times I saw Lindy seemed OK. But each contact gradually made me realize it was over. The relationship had died and I was beginning to mourn the loss of a relationship that had spanned all my adult life. Life began to look a bit pale.

It's OK to Be Weak

I continued feeling kind of low for awhile. Sandy went into the hospital and I stayed with her. I was really glad I was there. I felt like a real Dad. Lindy met me there and I felt the loss of "us." I wanted to touch, give her a hug, pick up our daughter and go home together. Did I really want Lindy or was I experiencing the draws of "family life" compared to the rigors of being "single?"

Seeing the therapist helped me clarify my decision to leave and get away from the put-downs and hurts. She said she thought I might be selling myself short by trading the hurts, anger, and jealousy for relief from loneliness. I told her how I'd come to hate the room I was living in, the cold, drab floors, the packing crates standing up in the corner. The place was really a garage after all, and bringing someone home to my place was embarrassing. The therapist took me through an exercise in which I visualized the room, the floor — cold, hard, bare, dirty. In my mind I asked the floor how we could get more comfortable together. The answer was to get *closer*. "See and feel me and you'll see I'm not so bad." I could do that in my mind, and my repulsion of the room seemed to change to acceptance. We were like two old friends who had done a lot of living. I also could see that I was not so bad and it was OK to be alone. I realized that a lot of my feelings of loneliness came from my attitude that if I were alone there must be something wrong with me. The hurts that separated Lindy and me would not have changed in four weeks. I resolved to continue the process to grow as a separate person and go on from there. I loved myself. That was something I hadn't felt in such a long while.

As things often happen, we are given the tools, seemingly by accident, to deal with whatever process life brings us. I was asked to put on a workshop on "Death and Dying" for people working in various agencies in the area. As I began reading Elisabeth Kubler-Ross again in preparation for the class, I was reminded that my purpose on earth was to grow to be me, to reach beyond my limits toward my future. Living with Lindy was once growth-enhancing. But finally, we restrained each other's growth. We decided to part, to make a contract with life rather than hold desperately to security. The decision was a good one.

Another blast of insight: Lindy was very much like my mother. Outwardly strong and self-sufficient, she had difficulty allowing herself to be vulnerable. She was not very accepting of weakness in others, particularly men. I realized that a lot of her support which I so praised — getting through school, — facing the draft and deciding to go to Canada, standing up to the mental health director — was support to be strong. Get out there and fight. When I said, "I'm tired of fighting, of being strong all the time. I want it to be OK if I'm weak," Lindy had difficulty.

I got into a hassle with Lindy the next Sunday over scheduling our time. She said she didn't want to feel she had to check in with me. I said that if I was going to be with the kids while she was gone I had a right to know when she was planning to return. I could see the "gameyness" of all this. We wanted to be free from each other, but not too free.

The next session with the therapist was good. I worked through a lot of feelings towards my mom and Lindy. I saw that Mom was scared of feelings and I learned that to feel was to abandon her in some way. When I "grew up" and met Lindy I realized I just traded my mom's barometer of what range of feelings was acceptable for Lindy's barometer. My earliest memory of Lindy and me was running on the beach in Santa Barbara, Lindy with wild abandon, me running slightly behind, somewhat stiffly trying to catch up, hoping that some of her playful ease would rub off on me. In the early months of our relationship I delighted in the thought that Lindy was "teaching me how to frolic." But still the focus of permission was always with her.

In the discourse with the therapist, I reclaimed my right to be free, to assert who I was, and let whatever felt right come out. I reclaimed the right to be my own barometer of acceptable feelings.

The End Teaches Love

Then came the day that would have been our 10th anniversary. I knew when we separated in May that by our anniversary in June I would have to be finally clear whether we would be together or apart. I knew I couldn't handle having our anniversary and still being in limbo. The day came and the relationship was over. It was the end of an era and the beginning of a new one. I cried my goodbye to Lindy in my new apartment. The tears flooded out and didn't seem to want to stop. I was aware now that with Lindy gone I felt the loss of a companion, lover, friend, partner, and mate, but I didn't feel the hole in me I had felt when she left me in college, or the hole I was afraid I'd feel then. I still felt whole. I was me and I was accepting more and more of me, reclaiming parts I'd lost or put down. I rejoiced in my naivete, my chauvinist jealousy and my anger over women's sexuality. I no longer had to hide parts of me, and that felt wonderful.

I celebrated our ending by going to San Francisco. I strolled through the streets and attended a street fair. I bought a painting which pictured a tiny castle way up in the air connected by a thin thread to a multicolored base with a quote from Thoreau: "If you have built castles in the air, your work need not be lost; that is where they should be. Now put the foundations under them." The hardest part of ending with Lindy was giving up the dream we had built together and somehow this little picture reminded me that I didn't have to give up the dream of a loving, free relationship, I just needed to continue building the ground work. I celebrated Father's Day alone and bought a Swiss army knife for the Dad in me from the Kid in me.

After taking Sandy to school, I had a daydream which became a meditation that was powerful. I returned to the memory of Lindy and Lenn together. I got back in touch with the sounds, the feeling of being trapped inside the camper, the revulsion and anger at my wife off fucking like an animal in the woods. I got in touch with my response of being passive, pleading, and tearful. That's how I had learned to hold onto the important woman (the mother) in my life — fall apart, be hurt, be needful. In my daydream I screamed with anger. I had the image of going out of the camper, picking up a rock and beating her head in, tearing off her breasts and mutilating her body. The image faded and I felt calm, somehow liberated from the past.

Later I realized that I couldn't directly express my anger at the loss of my central position in Lindy's life for fear that I would lose my only sense of support. My way of keeping Lindy was to become a jellyfish, which was an attempt to bind her and also to keep my strong destructive anger from coming out.

Much of the rage and hate I felt towards Lindy seemed to gradually disappear over the next few months. I began to appreciate her for the person she was, for the gift of life she brought into our relationship. I began to see that I was not a victim of circumstance, or a victim of Lindy, or Lenn. We had each played our roles perfectly. The anger still returned from time to time, usually at night when I was alone and couldn't get anything going with friends or females and felt sorry for myself. Most of the time, though, I felt very appreciative of Lindy and of me and of the love that was present in our good times as well as hard times.

One of my longest-held dreams had been to be a professor and have young students looking to me for understanding, working as part of a community of scholars who were all continually searching to understand ourselves and the world, creating a haven from the constant pressures of life, exploring issues of importance in quiet leisure in rooms of subtle elegance. Since graduating from the master's program in social work, I had thought of having a faculty position in a graduate school of social work where students combined personal growth with the attention of social change that was important in our increasingly perilous age of social unrest.

I didn't really believe that I would ever be in a position to consider the life of a professor, but many things in my life had changed. Almost on a whim, I applied for a position on the faculty of the Graduate School of Social Welfare at Sacramento State University. To my surprise, I was invited for an interview, first with a faculty committee, then with a student committee, and finally with the Dean and Assistant Dean. As I went through the interview process, I realized that the dream of a community of scholars was a myth out of my boyhood. I knew it was a myth, but it still felt sad to see the infighting and fear among the faculty and between the faculty and administration. I wondered whether I could fit in with another large bureaucracy, and if I really wanted to. My other dream was to go into private practice and create my own process for helping people and dealing with social issues. I felt I knew some things and could create a setting that would be unique and helpful.

I got the call from Sacramento State late one afternoon. My heart began pounding when I heard the voice of the Assistant Dean telling me I had been given an appointment on the faculty and I could begin work in two weeks. I'd been wondering since my last interview if I would take the position if it was offered, and in that moment all the considerations seemed to hang by a thread. This would be the big time. I liked the sound of the title, Professor Diamond. On the other hand, I would have to give up the dream of doing it on my own, creating my own unique process. In the interviews, I could see that the graduate school wasn't a hell of a lot different in its essence from the mental health system; it was just a higher-titled bureaucracy with the same preoccupation with paper work and money.

"I appreciate your offer for the position, but I've decided to continue my move into private practice." I felt relief and joy, a little frightened, but ready to move out on my own.

On My Own /Reclaiming Lost Parts

I met Mary at the nude beach in Santa Cruz. It was exciting to meet a new woman and I was pleasantly surprised when she suggested I call her the following weekend.

She invited me to stay at her house, and after a beautiful day of swimming and walking through the hills alone, I spent the evening with her, and then the night. It felt so nice to play, to experience a new woman without the constant fear and self-recriminations I had when Lindy and I were together. I guess "Open Marriage" worked best for me when I was single. I liked Merissa, Mary's daughter, and spent the weekend with them, playing with Merissa and making love with Mary. She asked me if I wanted to get high on some good grass and I had to admit I had only smoked once before and I wasn't sure I knew how. She reassured me that there wasn't anything to it. I didn't know if I got high, but the sex we had was mighty fine.

Looking back at the experience I realized that Mary was like Lindy when I first met her, kind of wild, playful, naive, needing a daddy to take care of her, but also very nurturing. Ah yes, and once she got hooked on me, I could get all the nurturing I needed. I could play daddy for a while then she could play mommy for the rest of the time. Shit, the game wasn't so fun once I saw how it was played.

I went to a Transactional Analysis group. The atmosphere was lousy, but I did meet some nice people. Sometimes I still got pretty lonely, but I had met women since Lindy and I split up and it was nice to begin experiencing what I really liked, and who I really was. Somehow over the years being married, I'd lost touch with what I liked. I realized again that I'd never enjoyed sleeping snuggled up with someone. I liked to touch, but when I was ready to sleep I wanted plenty of space and didn't like to be touched. Lindy was the opposite and I never accepted what my preference really was. It felt so freeing to tell a woman I'd been sexual with that I'd really prefer to sleep in my own bed or to have my space on the other side of the bed. I didn't have to apologize for my preference, and if the woman didn't like that, I could just say, "Fine, let's not continue seeing each other if the difference is that important to us." I was even seeing what kind of food I really liked. Somehow our tastes seemed to have become blended without my even noticing it.

I attended a weekend workshop on "Relationships" with Emily Coleman, which was a total turn on — one of those rare occasions when I was functioning at my peak. I was able to be exactly where I wanted to be, when I wanted to be. I would talk with a person, and be totally there, and as soon as I was finished I knew it immediately and could leave without any guilt and go on to where my energies were next. There was no effort, like a seal gliding through the water, I just flowed from one place to another. I felt a rare oneness, a total "rightness," about what I did. I could be free and open with people I had never met and say with real honesty what I wanted.

I realized how much of my interactions with people had become stereotyped and predictable. The ease of relating had turned into fear, always wondering how this or that action would affect someone. It had been a long time since I just overflowed with my own exuberant energy without any thought of how it looked to someone else. It felt great to feel again!

Two months after Lindy and I separated, I rented a camper and drove to Oregon. It was the first time since I was fancy-free in college that I'd taken a trip by myself, with no strings, no destination in mind — totally free and open to the world and myself. My first stop was a campground near Ashland. I had always wanted to see the Shakespeare Festival which is presented there every year. On the way to Ashland, I stopped and picked up a hitchhiker, a young man named Bill who was bright-eyed and "worldly wise" — like I was at age 20. We talked and shared our philosophy of life, our dreams for the future.

I met Marie at a campsite along the river that night. She was pretty, sexy, 19 years old, and tired of traveling with the guy she was with. She seemed quite amenable to teaming up with me, and I imagined wild nights of sexual pleasure with this blonde kitten from Washington. But when we talked, her interests seemed limited to the little cafe where she worked and the latest chemicals she had been stoned on. Somehow, I didn't feel much connection with her and decided I'd rather be with myself or Bill than have sex with someone I felt no other interest in. I couldn't quite believe my decision. It seemed I had dreamed of just such a scene for nearly half my waking hours from the time I was nine years old: being free on the road in a traveling bedroom with a beautiful, young blonde. But now, confronted with it in reality, it didn't look as good as I'd dreamed.

I felt free to give her a hug and drive on into town for the Fourth of July parade and picnic. Gazing across a group of conga players, I saw and felt a beautiful spirit, beautiful in body and soul. I could see it in her before we even talked. I walked up and introduced myself to Susan. She was lovely, full of sunshine, talented, alive, and warm. In a day we fell in love. Certainly there was passion, but it was the passion of being touched, of being open and vulnerable, and of loving her contact with others without feeling threatened. She was a little taller than me, and I felt the old discomforts — the taboo against being with anyone taller than my five-foot-five-inch frame — but we talked about it and joked and she kidded me, saying that I wasn't short where it counted. She was a little older, and I found the attractiveness of that too — she wasn't my stereotype of a young beauty, but I felt drawn to her nonetheless. It had been a long time since I had really loved and was loved. I'd forgotten how good it could feel, how complete. It was very different from meeting Lindy, though I loved Lindy too. At the best, our love had been beautiful and expansive, but it had become frightened in the last years and the extramarital sex had brought out insecurities. Now I was away on my own, growing and changing.

It was fun being an observer to my attractions. "Oh, that's interesting — you turn down the blonde bombshell who would have undoubtedly provided days and nights of sex and you're drawn to a woman you might not be sexual with but can be friends with." I didn't have anything to prove anymore or anyone to impress. I could just do whatever I damn well pleased.

The next night, we enjoyed a wild, passionate romp together. We laughed ourselves silly and covered each other with baby oil. I remembered when Lindy and I were that free. How far we had come since then. With Susan, I found the courage to be myself. I had never experienced someone who truly liked my body, or maybe I had never liked myself as much as I did now, coupled with a desire to experiment, to try new and "forbidden" experiences. We both really wanted to learn from each other and give to each other. Susan enjoyed my orgasms and I enjoyed giving them to her (helping her have them, that is — I knew we didn't give them to anyone anymore). It seemed so easy and natural, both in the sense of doing what we wanted and also in the other sense of being able to ask for what we wanted and having it given freely with love.

Although the relationship with Susan was short-lived, I learned a great deal about opening myself to my feelings and trusting myself — something I learned more about shortly afterwards.

TORI — Learning to Trust Myself

I met Harry and Lucy at a class I taught on "Alternative Lifestyles." I'd finally accepted that I was really teaching what I wanted to learn. Harry and Lucy interested me a great deal. They had been married for 12 years and had had an open marriage for the last seven. So far, my talks about open marriage as being a way to personal growth and growth as a couple were more theoretical than actual, since the practitioners of our little group were either divorced or considering it. But here was a real live couple who seemed very much in love and seemed to handle the jealous feelings with a minimum of stress. They talked about an organization called TORI (an acronym for Trust, Openness, Responsibility, and Interdependence), whose members were seeking ways to relate more openly and honestly with each other and to attempt to develop that magic ingredient, a loving community that so many of us seemed to be looking for. They said they'd let me know when the next TORI weekend was held. It sounded great to me and I was ready to attend.

Never, since my five-year involvement with Synanon, had I been so strongly affected by a community of people or felt my own release of power and energy so strongly. It was interesting too, since the two communities were so different in fundamental ways. While Synanon was autocratic and structured, TORI was totally democratic and unstructured. There were no leaders and the only guidelines were for people to be "totally themselves and to act on their own wishes rather than trying to please other people." Rather than chaos, the result was a free-floating, loving fabric of people who seemed to develop their own ever-changing process to hold things together. I was struck with the freedom people felt to leave the group, to return when they felt like it, to talk or be silent. I was also surprised at the open shows of affection, which ranged all the way from hugging each other to being openly sexual. Since everyone slept in one big room for the weekend, there was little privacy and whatever people did "in private" became part of the flow of the community. At first I was put off by this "fishbowl" existence, but I remembered reading about families in the 18th and 19th centuries living in large living spaces without the kind of separation and privacy that we have become used to. The result was that everything, including toileting functions and lovemaking, was not seen as private and hidden, and the result was a less inhibited group. So what the hell, I thought, I'd try it.

All went just fine for the first afternoon and evening. I met some really fine, loving people. I felt close to some men, even hugged a few that I liked. I shared my discomfort at being there alone for the first time with people who all seemed to know each other so well, and got lovely support and contact from one of the "old-timers." Everything was fine until night time, when I found myself sitting next to Jennifer, a beautiful young woman I had my eye on all evening. We were sitting on the back porch with the moon shining down, and I was feeling very romantic, with just the two of us alone in the world (though I was having trouble keeping that lovely fantasy going while people kept swirling around us, sitting at our shoulders, at our feet — someone was even sitting up against my back). Well, I was getting turned on, but I didn't quite know how one goes about asking someone to sleep with you in the open atmosphere of TORI. I'd always had a rising mixture of excitement and terror in similar situations in the past, as I got closer and closer to popping the question. But why not, what have I got to lose. "Jenny, I've..." Just then another guy sat down on the other side of Jennifer and started talking to her. Well, I was pissed. What happened to that old unspoken convention that you don't muscle in on another guy's girl once they're both starry-eyed and he's about to pop the question? I thought TORI was supposed to be a loving community — as I glared across at the intruder.

Well, shit, this wasn't the first time in my life I had been in such a situation, and I immediately launched into "Attack Plan A," which I always used when the "enemy" moved in on my action. First I moved a little closer to Jenny and put a hand gently on her shoulder to remind her who was there first and to let the intruder know I was in charge. Then I struck up a conversation with him, to let him know I was friendly and he could withdraw without my lording it over him. Next and most crucial in Attack Plan A was a quick but accurate assessment of the enemy's desirability as a mate for Jenny in this particular situation, as opposed to the desirability of yours truly.

Well, a quick perusal of the situation showed that he had me on height by at least five inches, but then I nearly always lose points in that category. His long hair indicated he was some kind of a hippie, so I knew I had him by a lot in status and success. I was clearly the most witty and intelligent, though he seemed to know Jenny from the past, which lost me a few points, and he seemed so damned comfortable and sure of himself I felt a little off balance. Well, I had the essential data for a decision. Do I move in with my scintillating intellect and "go for it," with guns blasting and pearly whites flashing, or do I excuse myself and leave. I had a moment's pause when I reflected that this might be a different environment than I was used to. Maybe here I could just come out openly and say, "Look Jenny, I feel drawn to you and I'd like us to spend the night together, but I'm also aware that Seth and you seem to have something going as well. Let's talk about how we're all feeling and maybe we can find some mutually agreeable solution that won't require me to blast that son-of-a-bitch out of the water or for me to get a hold of myself in the bathroom." Well the moment fleeted by and as Jenny got up to get a midnight snack, I moved quickly in with the question. It was all over, ladies and gentlemen, in less than a heartbeat. She said she had decided to sleep alone that night. Well, at least that long-haired hippie didn't win either.

I must say I never would have predicted that it would be Seth and me who had breakfast together the next morning and shared how we'd both felt the night before, and how we wanted to find some other way of relating to men so we didn't have to keep playing the Attack Plan A. We ended up hugging and spending a good deal of the weekend together. We obviously had the same taste in women, and for the first time in my life, I could enjoy being with a man without worrying about who was the most attractive and which one of us would score the most hits. It was a turning point for me in my own feelings about myself, about other men, and about the crazy things we do to ourselves in our games with women.

I went to the next TORI weekend hoping to have a sexual encounter, but didn't. I was beginning to notice that when I push too hard to get something like sex, the result was that I just pushed people away and I didn't get what I wanted. I lost touch with my own personal center and my energy was divided. When I stopped trying so hard to get something and was just myself, everything moved more smoothly.

The TORI people continued to offer real love and support. When people actively attempted to be more honest, when there weren't any leaders to set the agenda and take away responsibility from the people, when people did what felt right, the energy that got released was awesome.

Blanche let me cry out my loneliness, my need for strokes, my need to be liked, to be affirmed. Seth loved me and touched me and held me. Lucy slept with me, no sex, just loving, touching warmth. She let me comfort her in her hurts. It was so wonderful to have someone just come up behind you, wrap their arms around you, smile, and say, "I like you." Katherine had the hots for me, but was afraid. She told me I was beautiful (which I didn't quite believe, but liked hearing). I'd never thought of myself as good-looking. In fact, I'd never thought of myself as having much of a physical being at all. Somewhere along the way I learned that what counted in the world was to be successful and that success came from hard work and a quick mind. The right woman would come along to complement these attributes and you'd live happily ever after. Bodies were things that never worked quite right and needed to be washed periodically to keep wierd things from happening, like potatoes growing out of your ears. Lately, I'd been introduced to a totally new way of looking at things in the world.

North to Alaska

I spent the next weekend with my kids, Gene and Sandy, and though I still felt sick about leaving them, I enjoyed being with them. I felt much older that Friday night, for it was right after our final divorce hearing, a year and a-half after we separated. I began thinking about death. We all died, so the question was, how did we want to live? I felt I'd grown up in the past year. I was alone, death was real and inevitably ahead of me somewhere. I felt good, tired, but whole, and excited about the future.

I was given an opportunity to spend six weeks teaching at an isolated Air Force base in Alaska. I'd never really spent time alone by myself before. Ever since Lindy and I had been separated, there had been friends and lovers around. I thought I was ready to experience some real time alone, away from all the things I knew, just with me.

Six weeks with very little contact with women and without friends was almost too much. I thought my cock would fall off from masturbating so much. But the time alone, to think and read and reflect, was glorious.

I wrote a poem for the first time in my life, addressed to one of the few women I met in Alaska. I never thought I was creative but I liked the poem.

For Julie and Jed

Sometimes I touch a person before I touch them. With you it was so. Where was it that we touched? Are you a dream lover, a fiery illusion of long-hidden emotions — desires long stamped under the feet of white concrete goodness? You could be the red queen of my dream when my insanity comes forward to save my being from an eternity of white, white spaces. In between the lines I search for the life blood that is mine.

You're here and now, Julie. Your presence in my life is an affirmation of the life force that is in me — the deep, dirty, sexual energy that once was damned and damned and damned and damned, until . . . it froze.

I once was an iceman, cold and dry. To be so was to survive . . . to feel was to lose the only person who knew the key to *survival*. I will show you the key if you stay with me. I will show you the key if you stay with me. *I will . . . I will. I willllllllllllchill you* — must stay with me, please don't leave me, please, please please. I won't leave you mother — "Go, be a *man*. Get a wife. Go . . . Get . . . Go . . . get . . . *go . . . get.*"

But the *key*. Get a wife. But the *key* . . . Get a wife. But the *key* . . . Get a wife. But the *key*. Get a Wife. The *keywife.*

"Hello, my name's Jed." "My name's Lindy." I'll give it to you, if you give it to me. I've got the *key*. I'll set you free.

She gave me much, my wife of old, of times gone and past. She gave her youth, her touch, her pace in life . . . she helped me find success, to seek and find the top . . . she cared for me and loved me and wiped my tears and sent me back. The key I sought so long to find was not in her. She had it not to give.

When I said goodbye I thought just for a moment that I might die. She promised she'd give it to me. Damn it she promised. It isn't fair . . . but where, where, where . . . .?

Well you knew it all the time. The key's in me. Everyone can see that. But when it's dark and you haven't slept, and the bed is cold and your flesh cries out to be touched, and your friends are out, and the phone rings again . . . for someone else, and you're sick and your body aches, and you wonder if you'll ever feel good again, would you go if someone smiled and said I'll give it to you, if you give it to me?

I took long walks alone through the pure white snow. I thought about myself and my world.

I was unique, totally unlike anybody else and I was *fine* just the way I was. Elisabeth Kubler-Ross said it well, "Life is fullest when we realize that we are all snowflakes. Each of us is absolutely beautiful and unique and we are here for a very short time." Expressing the "me" as I found it was my mission on this earth. It was the finest gift I could give to myself and others. I was responsible for all that was me, my feelings, thoughts, actions. I created my own health and illness. "You don't hurt me. I hurt myself." I was not a victim of anything or anyone. I always had choices. The world was basically good and I could always get what I needed. There were no enemies I had to vanquish, only energy that I could use for my own and others' good — or to our detriment.

I had within me a center of being that, as I tuned into it, told me exactly what was in my best interest, and also in the best interest of other people, plants, animals, the whole cosmos.

This center was linked into a "cosmic control center" that likewise set an absolutely accurate direction (or flow) of how things should go. Sometimes I knew my decisions were right by looking "inside." At other times, the decision seemed to come from "out there."

Either way, this level of knowing went beyond my limited, rational mind, and connected me with a much deeper sense of my self.

LSD and Synanon

On my return from Alaska, I wanted to explore this newly discovered "deeper self." A friend suggested I try LSD which scared me at first. I thought I had been real daring trying marijuana for the first time. But LSD was something else. I remembered visiting the Mendocino State Hospital in the 60's when they were doing research about LSD, hearing sessions where people had beautiful, mystical experiences and could see beauty in the forms in an ashtry. I was drawn to try it for myself, to tap those realms of experience that were buried deep inside me — but another side of me said "no." What could possibly be so great about seeing beauty in an ashtry? I'd rather watch a sunset. And somewhere there was a deeper fear: "What might I find if I go deeply inside? I don't think I'll be one of those people who thinks he can fly and steps off the roof of a house, but what horrible fears might I confront? What would happen if I freaked out?"

I'd seen a friend a number of times while she was on

"acid," and she seemed to handle things fine. My reading convinced me that I didn't have to worry about genetic damage or brain damage or any permanent problems. Synanon just taught that drugs were unnecessary and better highs could be obtained without them. I remembered my Synanon "trip," and the non-drug psychedelic experience I had there, years before:

Fifty excited and somewhat frightened people arrived at the Synanon House in San Francisco at 8:00 o'clock on a Friday evening to begin our three-day "trip." All we knew in advance was that we would stay up until Sunday night and that people who had been on previous trips came out feeling totally ecstatic.

We changed our clothes and were given white robes to put on. We were led into a large room with pillows and soft lights. Soon guides, wearing multi-colored sashes around their necks, came in, and finally the "trip" directors appeared — a man and a woman wearing beautiful silk robes. The room quieted as the directors spoke. "You are about to embark on a journey, a trip of self-discovery. What you get out of the experience will depend on how willing you are to 'let go' of your fears and constraints. Each of you will get something very valuable, if you allow yourself. Good luck."

The next 48 hours were a blur of Synanon games, with yelling and screaming, movement, and theatre games, tears and touching. By early Sunday morning, we were exhausted, not sure whether we had gotten "it," but each in our own way closer to ourselves, closer to the fear that kept us from truly loving ourselves and making genuine contact with others. In the final hours, each person who was ready confronted their own private fears and went beyond them. For me, I confronted my 'good boy' way of being in the world, always helpful but rarely honest. Somehow if I could just convince you how good I was, you'd love me. The image broke in a torrent of tears and it seemed as though my whole being was wrapped up in that image. This is me and it's being destroyed. I cried and wailed and out of the hopelessness of it all I reached out to the people in my group in a new, more honest way.

As the last group ended and the 50 people reassembled in the room that we had left only 48 hours previously, there was a feeling of renewal and rebirth, a very deep joy. Addicts and "squares," young and old, had shared a trip of profound simplicity. The directors reminded us that we would not stay in the "high" state we were now experiencing. We would return to our regular lives, but this trip, this passage would be a lifelong reminder of what we are each like when we allow fear to drop away and experience our true loving selves.

As 50 shouting, laughing, crying people burst out into the main Synanon ballroom amidst cheers and claps from hundreds of people who had already experienced a "trip break," I knew that the experience would always be a guiding force in my life. Without any drugs I had been transported to another realm of existence, a deeper, more loving, more connected space within myself.

Now as I contemplated taking my first "drug" trip, I wondered whether I would return to that same world of gentle love.

Even with all my "professional" experience with drugs, my personal experience had been very limited. Occasionally, I would have wine with dinner, and I would drink enough to get a little buzz on at an occasional party. One time after graduation I drank enough to enjoy the experience of walking zig-zag through the park at midnight and falling in a heap into the middle of the other partyers sitting around a campfire keeping warm. I had to stop twice at each stop sign driving home because I kept seeing two red lights, one above the other. My "hard drug" experience consisted of eating marijuana brownies made specially for Lindy and me by my graduate students, who couldn't believe we'd never been "high" but were happy to introduce us, even though I had to admit that I'd never smoked anything in my life and was sure I would make a total ass of myself if I tried to learn at their party.

So there I was, looking rather skeptically at a quarter-inch square piece of paper with a purple flower in the center that my friend was trying to convince me was LSD. "I know this sounds stupid, but what do I do with it?"

"Just put it on your tongue and chew it up. You'll start feeling the effects in about 15 minutes."

I did a quick meditation to quiet my fears, prayed to the powers that be for a safe trip, and for whatever enlightenment was waiting for me. We each placed the tab on our tongues and sat on the floor with the sun streaming in my kitchen window. It was a warm, beautiful day. At 10:00 it was already warm, but it didn't look like it would be too hot. The birds were singing happily and I felt very much at peace with the world.

I first noticed that my body was feeling tingly, and I relaxed and watched the sunlight making lovely patterns on the floor. Gradually the feelings spread throughout my body and everything seemed heavy but comfortable. I definitely felt "strange." Everything seemed intensified and I would find myself staring at some object in the room and then some little detail on that object and somehow the spot on the chair that I'd never noticed before became very interesting. As I watched it, it seemed to change shape and seemed to melt, then the chair would seem to melt and everything seemed somehow different, though I could still see it in the same old way just by blinking my eyes and "seeing things the way they are." It was as though I could move at will from one state of consciousness to another. I could look at my friend and she was herself, just as I had remembered her at 9:00 a.m. before the trip, but the more I would look at her face, the more it would change and flow into an animal face, then a witch, then an angel. I didn't feel afraid and there was no judgment, such as "this is good or bad, or right or wrong." It all just flowed by. As I watched her face I felt at times as though we were separate beings and at other times like we flowed together, and somehow it felt like we were one being. I remembered that feeling from my Synanon trip. There was no feeling of time passing and I just enjoyed watching the faces change. Just as suddenly as I had gotten interested in the faces, I got interested in something else. It was the most incredible feeling of freedom, with no disjoining as usual when I change attention from one thing to another or one person to another. There was no sense of loss or excitement of discovery, just a new "isness" that flowed into awareness.

We got silly with each other and rolled around on the carpet laughing and tickling each other, like two little puppies with no cares in the world. The play turned into sexual excitement and we began making love. The experience was very, very nice. When I was inside her vagina, there was no feeling of having to "work at anyting," no thoughts of orgasms, no feelings of "what feels right for me or what would she like," just a constant rising energy flowing easily between us. As I looked down at my trip mate, she seemed to change into a goddess, then I'd blink again and she'd be a man which struck me as being very funny and I started to laugh, then she looked like me and I felt like a woman. I couldn't tell if she had the penis and it was in my vagina or if I had the penis inside her. That felt strange, but not the least bit uncomfortable. As the excitement got higher and I got more "turned on" the feeling of being two separate people lessened. It wasn't as if there was an "I" that was making love with a "her" but just an "I-thou" that was flowing with energy, and yet there was no feeling of "losing myself." When I got close to orgasm it was as if I stayed right on the edge forever, without trying to "hold it back" as I used to do so often. The more thrusting and movement there was, the more I just seemed to stay at that incredibly high plateau right on the edge of orgasm. When I finally did have an orgasm, it seemed to come out of nowhere. It was like a gentle explosion that totally consumed everything, as if I disappeared for a moment and then returned with new vitality.

Later as I went to the bathroom I became entranced with the toilet. It seemed to be a very special thing to me all of a sudden. No longer just a hole to deposit waste, but a terribly interesting "thing" to talk to and play with. It was like being a little kid again and finding total delight in objects that adults thought were uninteresting. I touched it and talked to it, and examined in minute detail the way the sides curved down and around the floor. Somehow, this all struck me as incredibly funny and I began laughing and laughing, harder and harder, like in those rare moments when you laugh so hard your sides hurt and you pee in your pants and tears roll down your cheeks. Most of us spend most of the time of our lives getting away from pain and rarely "go for the delight." This seemed like a reminder to me that there was so much more available to us, and it was as close as the nearest toilet.

Later I decided to take a walk alone outside the house. As I walked I felt as though I was partly in a dream. Everything was as I remembered it. There was still the front lawn, somewhat brown. The white picket fence still ringed the house. Everything still looked typically suburban. The trees were green. The children played in the streets. And yet everything was also different. My body certainly felt different now very strange and tingly. As I walked farther down the street toward the grammar school, I felt an increasing sense of peace and calm. I felt connected to the streets and sidewalks and the trees and flowers in a way that I rarely felt in my ordinary conscious existence. As I got close to the school, I saw a boy throwing a boomerang. I'd never seen anyone actually use one before. It seemed beautiful to me. Out it would go, away and away, and all of a sudden it would turn in midair and return to the boy, landing close at hand. As I watched, I felt an understanding of life I had not had before. Life was a moving away from a central beginning, but the return was as sure as the leaving. There was a oneness and we were all connected to it, and we knew it through our experience. Love was the energy that ran through this connection. It was comforting somehow to know that the experience on the drug was not so different from my Synanon experience without drugs. It seemed to solidify and deepen the experience for me and to remind me that there are some universal truths and they're in us — not in the drug. The drug acts only as a stimulus, as a guide to that realm.

Two years after we separated, I still felt a strong connection with Lindy. Although I never asked directly, I always seemed to know what was going on in her life.

I babysat one night and when she returned she seemed open and caring toward me and wanted me to stay and smoke some grass. I said OK and gave her compliments that seemed honest, but made it clear I wasn't interested in getting involved sexually. Although I still felt some sexual attraction, I knew that getting involved would complicate our relationship. I couldn't go toward her and away from her at the same time.

A week later, Lindy and I got together again. She'd been sick and seemed genuinely sorry that my plans for my next job had fallen through. We definitely related better in times of mutual adversity than when one of us was feeling good. We resolved that I would spend more time with Gene and Sandy, and be more responsible for them. She'd been feeling boxed in with the children, feeling hurt and angry that this "parenting stuff" had begun as an equal sharing between us, but then she was having to carry most of the load by herself. She was seeing the world as negative, seeing people as hostile, and she generally felt hopeless. I could listen and hear her and see how different our views of the world were. For the first time in a long while, I could allow myself to feel her pain, and hold her and genuinely let my feelings out to comfort and care for her — and yet I had to answer her question about us by telling her I thought we wouldn't get back together. For me, there was no going back to the days before the end. It all had to happen as it did. I was glad in some way. I had learned much about myself in the process. I had needed to break through the fear of losing her, of being on my own, and I had done that, even though it meant our relationship had to end. I couldn't continue to grow as long as that fear was there. I had to go toward the fear and move through it before I was free of it.

Yet that night I thought seriously about getting back together with Lindy. But the more I thought about it the more I knew that the process of my own growth, of getting to know myself, what I liked, what I needed, had to continue. I fought like hell to keep the fear of separation from becoming a reality, but now that I'd faced it, I felt I had to ride it through to the end and see where this path led. I still felt the pull of our togetherness, particularly when Lindy seemed so loving and I felt so lonely. It would be so much easier to see Gene and Sandy more often, rather than always having to "work it out." And yet I knew I would continue to separate our lives.

Lindy said she was tired of scrimping on the little money I was sending and suggested that I take the children to live with me full time. At first, the thought of being a full-time father scared me. But later, while I was running and thinking about my class on decision-making and coping skills, it occurred to me that either choice with the children would be just fine. Either way would be a win for me and the children. When I realized that I could feel fine with either choice, I felt very free and happy. I didn't feel ruled by the fear of either having the children or not having them. Now I could think about options, knowing that whatever we decided would work out OK.

Chapter Six

I Am As Deep As Creation

The Myth of Masculine Privilege

Early in the fall, I met my friend Patrick, and we both attended a workshop with Herb Goldberg on "The Hazards of Being Male." What he said rang true for me from my experiences as a man. There has been so much talk about the negative affects of sexism on women, as though men always had it so great, but we *all* pay a terrible price being "men" and "women." Even though men have had easier access to power and prestige, we also die sooner and contract every major disease at rates of two to six times more often than women. We kill ourselves with booze and suffer the slow death of going through life cut off from our feelings. I'd still been living with the training of thinking that I had to deny pain in order to be a man. My hero was the guy on my high school basketball team who played a whole game on a broken ankle. I'd learned so well to disregard my body that I had to get very sick before I even knew something was wrong. Women were being more open about what they enjoyed sexually, and I had to admit that I wasn't aware enough of my own body to know what I really liked, beyond the fantasies I had learned out of the pages of Playboy Magazine. It had been damn frustrating to be with "liberated" women who were willing to tell me what they liked sexually, in explicit detail. "I want you to touch me like this, and kiss me this way, and if you rub this direction it feels good, but the other direction tickles, and kissing my toes drives me wild, and the backs of my knees turn me to butter, and the insides of my arms put me in heaven, but my breasts are sensitive, sometimes I like it and sometimes I don't . . . . Now be sure to tell me what you like and what you don't like." I felt like a fool. I didn't even know.

As we sat in the audience listening to Goldberg, I felt a weight being lifted from my body. Someone was finally putting into words the deep feelings and thoughts that I didn't even know I had.

I realized I felt compassion for the plight of women as they had become more verbal in attacking the beliefs that restricted them to the roles of housewife and mother and sexual object. I kept feeling "yes and yes and yes you're right, things have been tough for women and you've got a right to be angry, and I should learn to change the diapers and do the dishes and iron my own clothes, and be concerned with your pleasure as well as my own." And I kept shoving down the little voice that kept exploding *"How about me?* I haven't had it all so fucking good, and yes I'm tired of spending my life working while you stay home with the kids, and tired of constantly fighting for some shred of humanity in a world that only cares if you produce. I'm tired of being strong all the time, and of fighting my depressions that make me want to give up and go to sleep forever. I'm tired of watching my friends drink more and more, and running from the fear that I'll say, 'fuck it,' and drive my car into an embankment like Gary did awhile ago, and I'm tired of hiding the rage I felt when all I heard for weeks afterward was about poor Carol who has to carry on with two small children. And it frightens me to know the rage is so strong that if I let myself feel anything at all, I'll want to kill someone, and what's worse nobody knows and there's no way to break through the walls of steel I've covered myself with to let you know how fucking lonely it is inside."

But there stood Herb Goldberg saying things that let me know that he knew. And I said to myself, "If he knows what it's like inside this bomb shelter, others must know too. If he can talk about what it's like and how I got inside, I know there must be a way out."

I began reading the work of Abraham Maslow again. His psychology of people was so loving and positive. Our needs for love and esteem can be met, he said, as we continue to develop our infinite human potentials.

What I liked about Maslow was that he was so positive, so supportive. So much psychology I had read told us all the things that could go wrong with us frail humans, but nothing about what people could be at their best. I'd felt like I'd spent my life looking for all the "problems" in my life so I could "get rid of them" and become healthy. I'd accepted that life was painful, a constant struggle to stay on top of things or I'd be engulfed by the surging tide of my unconscious shit.

In Maslow's philosophy, we don't have to struggle so much. He believed we all had a unique "central core" of being that was not bad, but neutral or good. All we had to do was allow ourselves to reconnect with that core, allow it to guide us and our lives could become more harmonious and happy. It also gave us a way to decide upon our values, what was right for each of us and what was wrong.

I'd always been uncomfortable about how to guide my behavior. Clearly my parents didn't have all the answers. Religious beliefs seemed based more on practicality than basic wisdom — how else could I justify all the religious wars that have been fought? Kill for Christ? The philosophers I read in college didn't seem any clearer about a system of beliefs that could guide human behavior, whether we lived in Russia or the U.S., in the 16th century or in the 20th.

Maslow said there was a way to know and we all had access to that knowledge. By learning to be guided by this inner core, we could have a consistent measure of right and wrong action. I loved that idea, but what bothered me was trying to figure out how I was supposed to find this "inner core" of wisdom. Maslow suggested that it could not be found through the intellect, trying to find it with the head.

He implied that it was found by tuning into the feelings, the more subtle energies coming from the body. There was the rub. Though I could certainly say I had a body from a very early age, I couldn't say I really knew it very well.

While growing up, the emphasis was so heavily placed on thinking and talking and reasoning that I think I had the idea of Jed Diamond as being a brain on top of a broom stick. The only time I was really aware of my body was when it hurt or when I was sick, or when I was masturbating and then I wasn't aware so much of my body as I was of just my cock. I'd begun more recently to develop a whole new attitude about my body. Instead of seeing it as something to ignore, as a handy pedestal to support my brain or an unruly child to be whipped into place when it misbehaved, I was beginning to see my body as a friend, as part of me. I was seeing that if I listened closely, my body would tell me accurately the state of my well-being. When it was sick, it was telling me to tune in and see what was out of balance in my life; it was *not* telling me to quickly make this fucking cold go away so I could get back to my work.

Looking at my body in this new way even taught me about mechanical devices like cars, which always scared me because I didn't understand them. They didn't talk so I'd never been able to relate to them. Driving home late one night, I noticed that one of the red lights on the dash was flashing. I pulled over to see what the problem was, but realized I didn't have the slightest idea where to begin to find out. I was tired and frustrated and wanted to get home and go to bed. I finally gave the damn light a smack with my fist. I felt a rather perverse delight when the light went out. I drove home, humming a rakish tune, thinking, "I don't care what the mechanic tells me in the morning, as far as I'm concerned the car is fixed."

I realized that was the way I had always treated my body. If it hurt or I had a fever, I took aspirin as quickly as I could to make the symptoms go away so I could get on with my life. It never occurred to me to see what my body was trying to tell me.

I began doing a meditation whenever I started to feel sick, and I "asked" my body what it was trying to tell me. I felt foolish when I began — what would people think if I told them I talked to my stomach — but what I heard when I listened made it all worthwhile. I've had stomach problems since I was a kid. As an adult the doctors always thought I was about to get an ulcer. I drank Maalox like milkshakes and always carried tablets with me. Now when my stomach begins to hurt I ask, "What's the message you want me to get?" Recently it told me I was under increasing stress and I needed to relax or I would get cancer. Believe me, I listened and cut back on my work. It consistently tells me to slow down, to eat more slowly, usually to do everything more slowly. I had always accepted stomach problems as part of being a man. I certainly don't anymore.

I began reading about stomach problems in the *Well Body Book*. From that it seemed clear that intense, sustained anxiety, hostility, and resentment produce increased stomach acid, which in turn produces small lesions in the mucous lining of the stomach. Once this sensitivity is induced, hemorrhages are produced by the "most trifling traumas." Contact of gastric juice irritates the membranes further, resulting in accelerated secretion of acid and further engorging of the lining. Prolonged exposure of lesions to acid produces an ulcer. So it made sense to me to continue taking antacids at times of stress as well as vitamins to help repair the damaged lining in my stomach, and to see what I was doing that contributed to the anxiety and hostility.

The book also talked about the unconscious features of stomach problems. There is often an *unconscious* need to be taken care of, along with a *conscious* drive for independence. Repressed wishes to be loved, nurtured, and taken care of express themselves in physical symptoms. It explained that the first form of being cared for and loved that we experienced was being nursed, and the sensations of being both loved and fed became emotionally associated for the rest of our lives. If the wish to be loved, as one was by the mother, is denied gratification, the associated tendency to want to be nourished is energized. All this fit well with what stresses seemed to be going on with me.

I'd always been outgoing and independent, but had felt at times like crawling up in someone's arms and just being held. That feeling had always scared me. My independent side said I didn't really want that, and I felt a deeper fear that I wouldn't ever want to go out in the world again if I ever allowed myself to retreat to the warmth of a woman and let myself be taken care of.

I'd learned that colds and flu were messages that I needed to rest, though I still had to fight the feeling that I should be well in a short time, as if I was allowed only a certain amount of time off. I often felt like life was a big basketball game. To win I had to run from the first whistle to the last. We were allowed a few two-minute time outs along the way, but no one could ask the referee to extend the time out to three minutes because we needed a little longer to rest.

I always saw life as a team sport. Being alone was cowardly and not even in the rules of the game. In all the years with Lindy, I never felt free to take time for myself. I always felt I had to be doing something useful. I even decided that I went to all those dull evening meetings for my job because it was the closest I could get to being alone, and still feel I could justify my actions.

Sleep was also a suspect activity, only to be engaged in if the purpose was to get you ready for the next day. Sleeping late on Sunday was acceptable only because by God I'd earned it by driving myself all week, and I needed my rest to fight the new wars on Monday. I learned early on to "never, never, never be caught sleeping at unauthorized times!" I couldn't even count the times that Lindy would come in while I was dozing in a chair or sacking out on the couch in the early evening. I would rouse myself as soon as I heard her footsteps. "Were you sleeping, hon?" "Oh, no, just resting my eyes." I even remember being wakened from a sound sleep at midnight and finding myself feeling guilty, saying cheerfully, "No I wasn't asleep, I was just reading."

I can't believe I lived with such insanity for so long. I still tell my wife I feel fine driving even when I'm dead tired, but I've been working on that one too. It's felt like a very long road, but I was glad I began to listen to what my body was telling me, and began to be strong enough to act on what I was hearing.

Cock Sure /The Wisdom of the Penis

The discomfort I felt when I'd piss was another lesson in listening to my body. It began shortly after Lindy returned from her trip to South Dakota with Dena, although I didn't see the connection at the time. I also felt some discomfort when Lindy and I made love.

It was so vague I wasn't even sure it was real. I couldn't really remember how it felt when I would come in the past, but in some way it didn't feel as good as it had. I saw Dr. Roberts several time and got all kinds of different medications for the infections. I asked him if the infection could be affecting my sexual response, but he seemed a bit uncomfortable and said he didn't know. For some reason I didn't feel comfortable talking about it with Lindy. She seemed to be enjoying herself just fine since she got back from South Dakota.

I'd always trusted doctors to know what they were doing, but I was beginning to wonder about Dr. Roberts. He'd been giving me one medication after another and nothing seemed to be helping. Finally he suggested a "small" operation to remove part of my prostate gland which would clear things up. The thought of being cut into scared the shit out of me. When I suggested to him that I'd like to get another opinion, he seemed offended, although he told me to go ahead if I didn't trust him.

I went to the medical library at the hospital and read what I could find about prostate trouble. I found it was generally more prevalent in older men, though it could be a problem at any age. What really scared me was a line that said viewing the prostate under the scope was a tricky business. Many physicians who were inexperienced would make the mistake of saying the prostate was enlarged when in fact it was not. I had this image of Dr. Roberts, who had done most of his work with older men, thinking "now I've got a young one I can try out my new toy on and see how it works." What scared me the most was knowing that I had come close to trusting the "doctor" over my own intuition because he was a "specialist" and must know the best thing for me.

I finally went to a different urologist, feeling a little guilty to have deserted Dr. Roberts. To my relief and surprise, Dr. Evert took me off all the medications. The burning and discomfort disappeared after a few weeks, leaving only the vague feeling that my ejaculation wasn't as strong. Dr. Evert acknowledged that he didn't know much about sexual problems and referred me to a specialist in San Francisco. For once, one of these goddamned doctors had been honest enough to say "I don't know" instead of getting out his knife to cut the problem away.

I met with Dr. Finkle in San Francisco, a specialist on urology and sex. He was very straight with me. He told me he could make a lot more money doing surgery than talking to people about their sexual problems, so he needed to be paid in advance. There was no guarantee that my sexual relations would improve, but after one session we could decide together whether to go on. He did a complete physical with real gentleness, unlike my other doctor, who seemed to delight in watching me cry out when he stuck his finger up my ass to "massage the prostate." Finkle seemed reassured when I told him that neither of us had an affair during this time when our sex had been so unsatisfying. I told him I'd been having the prostate trouble for about a year, and he seemed interested in what was going on in my life during that time. "Nothing that I can think of," I told him. His prescription was simple, almost too simple for a $50-an-hour specialist. "Drink two gallons of water a day to flush out your system, then have no sex for two weeks. When you do have sex again make the setting romantic and conducive to good lovemaking."

"Jesus, doc, I can handle everything except the two gallons of water a day. I won't ever be able to leave the bathroom." He just smiled and said to do it. He said not to worry if our lovemaking didn't improve immediately, but to give it a little time. After a year of urinary discomfort, disinterest in sex, unsatisfying sex when I would come almost before I could get my cock inside, and anger and impatience from Lindy, I was ready to try anything.

"Give it a try and come back in two months," he said. I left the office with more hope than I'd felt in a long, long time.

After seeing Dr. Finkle I began to wonder if anything had happened during the time I was having "problems." It began to dawn on me that there was a connection between my problems with my cock and my feelings about the events in my life over the past year. When I began thinking about it, it was all so obvious. Of course there was a connection. After Lindy returned from her trip I felt much more pressure to perform. I needed to keep pace with the unknown men she may have met — men I was too afraid to ask about.

In my fear I had deadened my feelings. But my cock wasn't dead and it had been expressing my inner feelings all along. "I'm scared. Lindy returns from her trip all excited and wants to be more sexual and wants me to do it more often. I'm not sure what this is all about and I'm not sure I want to 'do it bigger and better'. I'm not even sure I like sex as much since she's become more aggressive. She calls it 'premature ejaculation'; I call it 'I want to get this over with as quickly as possible'. Now she wants to act on that 'head tripper' Jed's idea to have an 'open marriage'. Well, let me tell you. Your head may think you want an open marriage, but take it from someone who is closer to the center of things. Your cock knows you don't, and you're scared shitless. And what thanks do I get for having the guts to speak out? They want to cut a little bit out of me. I ought to just keep my head down and my little mouth shut.

It took a long time before I was ready to hear what my cock was trying to tell me. For years, I had been thinking about having a vasectomy. It had been clear to me for some time that I didn't want to father any more children by design or by accident, and I wanted a form of birth control that I could count on. I couldn't justify telling myself it was the woman's responsibility any longer. Yet, since Lindy and I had been in an open relationship and had been sexual with other people, I had had two pregnancy scares and one actual pregnancy. When I read the letter saying she was sure that the night we made love was the night she conceived, I was terrified. What would this mean for my life? What did she want from me? I breathed a sigh of relief when I continued reading and found that she was happy she was pregnant, wanted nothing from me, and that she and her boyfriend had decided to have the baby and put it up for adoption. Then I felt hurt. There would be a child I helped conceive somewhere in the world and I'd never have a chance to know her. Somehow, I even knew it would be a girl.

I read everything I could find on vasectomy and talked to friends who had them. I knew in my head they were safe, relatively painless, and easy. What it got down to was my terror at the thought of being cut into. When I realized that was the fear, I did a meditation, feeling somewhat foolish, and asked my cock what it thought about having a vasectomy. The answer I got was to go ahead and have it done. It was right for me.

A week later, I was sitting in the waiting room of the doctor's office. I had taken the tranquilizer he had prescribed two hours before. I was still terrified, but drowsy. I brought my mother along for moral support and to drive me home afterwards. I knew I wasn't one of those macho men who would jump back on his Harley afterwards and ride off looking for someone to try it out on. I planned to take the weekend plus Monday off if I needed it and just lie in bed and take care of myself.

I went into the doctor's inner office with him and the nurse, pulled down my pants and I got up on the table. The air was cold where I'd shaved myself in preparation for the "operation." The actual procedure was minor, even for someone like me who was terrified of doctors, and particularly doctors with knives. The tranquilizer had made me drowsy. The shots into my balls were much less painful than I was sure they would be, certainly less than novocaine in the mouth. I couldn't even feel the two little cuts in my scrotum, and within half an hour I was walking proudly, though a bit gingerly, back to the waiting room.

The healing went quickly. I took the extra day even though I felt fine, wore a jock strap as directed to give the added support I needed. Two weeks later I returned, shot a specimen in a tube, and they confirmed that I was "shooting blanks." Shortly thereafter, I tried it out for the first time, with a little trepidation that it wouldn't work right. It felt great, and I had the added bonus of being told that my come tasted better than before.

Passive Man, Wild Woman and Beyond

I kept trying to keep everything under control. At times, it felt as though I was handling things OK; at other times, I felt I was on the brink of disaster. I thought if I could just keep calm, think everything through, I would be all right. But there seemed to be so much to think about — trying to establish my work, being alone, relating to children, going to court, meeting new women.

I had a dream one night that disturbed me. I saw Lindy and Jim, nude, playing with each other and teasing me. I felt the suppressed rage that I remembered so well from the past and felt impotent at not being able to do anything. I finally shot a blow dart that would make her itch, but I did it in such a way that she wouldn't know who did it. I felt alone. Where's a woman for me? I wanted to fight Jim, but I didn't.

Sandy was in the hospital again for surgery on her palate and I was glad I could be there to comfort her. I was definitely better dealing with her emotional needs than with her physical pain. I'd been trying to take care of myself, and to deal with Lindy's jabs about my lack of caring as a father without feeling guilty. It was still hard, but little by little and bit by bit, I felt stronger and more sure of myself. It felt so difficult to talk to Lindy that I would feel myself get cold whenever we interacted. I wrote her a letter, trying to reach out to her:

Dear Lindy,

When I'm with you I find I try to protect myself behind a shell of intellectual indifference which isn't at all the way I feel. Yesterday, as I often feel with you, I wanted to get out of there as fast as I could, to get away from the constant criticism I feel when I'm around you. Through my eyes I always feel criticized no matter what I do. I guess through your eyes I appear totally indifferent and irresponsible, trying to get out of as much as I can.

I felt a touch of warmth when you gave me the sweatshirt. It seemed that underneath the hurt and anger you were saying, "You're still the father of our children, and I care about you."

The whole court thing is strange to me. I tell myself that we tried to work things out together and we couldn't, so we have to let the adversary process work its course. I keep thinking that if I could just understand what's going on with you and if you could really hear me, we could do what's right for all of us. But for now that won't happen. We're both too guarded to listen. I'll be glad when things are over tomorrow and we all know where we stand. Tomorrow is set up for a win/lose at best, though probably we'll both lose. I think of better futures for us, where we can be more real with each other, and help each other be parents to Gene and Sandy.

I wish you well.

Jed

It had been a year since the night I left the house to stay with Dale. It had been a year of change and growth for me. I'd gotten older and more "myself." That was an important step for me, to have the courage to begin again to risk being myself, and risk losing my lifeline. I did take that risk though, and found that I didn't need a lifeline tied to a woman anymore. I had myself and I had friends, and I could get what I wanted out of life.

I went to the nursery school Sandy attended. I'd been able to get straight with Lindy about kid stuff and it felt good to feel my own power, and not get hooked into feeling guilty. I also felt a little lonely. I realized that stopping the game we'd been playing and assuming responsibility for myself made me alive and free, but I also lost the comfort of having some relationship with Lindy, even though it had been bad. I was beginning to really feel that it was over with her, after a year, and it felt good but also very lonely. I kept getting feelings of wanting a woman, but knew I'd rather be alone than just have any woman. The person I wanted was very special and I was willing to wait for the right person to come along.

I met Sheila at a weekend TORI gathering. I had told myself I wasn't going looking for women. This was going to be a family weekend with my children, where I could relax with friends and meet new people. Seeing her walk into the swimming pool changed all that. I felt the sparks flying and that lovely warm feeling spread through my groin. When we talked, we couldn't seem to stop. I liked everything about her, but most of all I was drawn to her excitement and energy. Going through the separation and divorce seemed to drain my life energy. With Sheila, I felt strong again.

It only set me back a moment when she told me that she had just gotten out of a monogamous relationship that had smothered her and she was clear that any serious relationship would have to be open. I was just as clear that I had just gotten out of an open relationship that had drained me, and though I wouldn't rule out an open relationship in the future, I was clear that any serious relationship for me now would have to be monogamous. I felt strong stating my position and listening to hers. Here was a powerful woman, making her own living, with her own goals in life, who could match my strength. I loved the energy I felt as we flowed together through the weekend. She related well to my children, my work, and my plans for the future.

By the end of the weekend, we were talking about spending the rest of our lives together, then laughing that we didn't know each other that well. We agreed to learn what we needed to know to decide whether or not we would spend the rest of our lives together. I drove home in a cloud singing all the love songs I knew. I couldn't wait to get home so I could write her and share my new-found love.

Dear Sheila,

I know you know where I've been since we departed at the gate yesterday because we've been together. God I feel your presence totally. We've never been apart since we met. You've done and been everything with me — inside, outside, above me, around me, through me, beside me, along me, against me, on top of me, under me. I love you Sheila.

Somewhere inside me there's been a seed of knowledge of what it would be like to be with you. Not really a longing, but a deep, deep spring of potential life flow. I've known it's been there for a while now and that it would only be tapped by a strong, powerful force that was deeply loving. I am an incurable romantic and I do believe that I have special power in the universe to bring about the things I desire. But I also know about people and our uncanny ability to push away and destroy the very things that sustain life. All of which is to say I knew I'd find you and I also knew I might never meet you.

But goddamn it, I could never have guessed the way that part of me would manifest itself. It's like riding a volcano when we're together. Our energy shakes me to the core. It's impossible to stop looking at you. All my buttons are pushed. All are on all the time. When we're apart the energy flows out into the world and enriches everything it touched. Jan was bathed in it all the way home from TORI. Gene and Sandy were dipped. The mountains and valleys felt it. I can't wait to see you again.

Love, Jed

I enjoyed making the 90-mile drive from the San Joaquin Valley to San Francisco to see Sheila. Once again, life had a purpose, I had a place to go, a person to move towards. The weekends with Sheila were hot. We talked non-stop. We made love a lot. We played in the sun and played in the City. We drank a lot of wine and smoked a lot of grass. Sheila was a whirlwind. By the time I got home late Sunday night I was exhausted. After a few weekends like that I realized I needed five days to recover from the energy I expended in the two I was with Sheila.

There were times I felt I was riding on her energy, times her energy seemed to drain me, and times I felt renewed by her. I knew I felt carried along by it all, but I liked it. Sheila talked about wanting to live together, wanting me to move to the Bay Area. When I was with her it sounded good. When I'd get back home, I'd be sure I wasn't ready to live with her. When I was driving half-way between, I felt 50-50.

I finally told her I didn't want to leave the Valley at that time since I wanted to give my private practice more of a chance to flourish, but I encouraged her to come and get a place near me and see how she liked living in my neck of the woods. I reasoned that we could then see if we wanted to live together. She said I was putting her through an obstacle course and my desire to go slowly showed I wasn't committed to the relationship. I didn't like hearing that and I tried to reassure her that I was committed. She was the woman for me. I just needed to go at my own pace.

Alone in my room, I tried to sort out my feelings. "When I'm with Sheila, it's hard to know what I feel. My feelings seem to merge with hers. I have such a history of trying to please people, and when Sheila says 'you don't seem committed, you don't seem to love me as much as I love you', I feel an incredible pull and I want to show her again and

115

again how much I love her. Where is the boundary between loving another person completely, and giving yourself away?"

Having space and time to myself has always been an important way to maintain my own identity. Yet over the years with Lindy, I found it more and more difficult to find time to be alone. The more I would try, the more demanding she seemed to be that I wasn't around enough. I'd always end up feeling she was right. The only time I could be alone without feeling guilty was when I was working.

With Sheila, I was able to take my own space, but wasn't able to be nose-to-nose with her and say, "I hear your fear, but I'm not going to buy into it." Part of my need to be away from her during the week was that I wasn't yet aware enough and secure enough to always stand up for myself when I was with her. Damn, I hated to admit it. When I was with Lindy, I gradually gave up bits and pieces of myself over the period of 10 years that we were married. In the year after we separated, I reclaimed a lot of my power, my self, my desires and sureness about my own needs and rythms. But how much power did I really express when I felt under pressure from a strong woman? It definitely was in relationship with a woman that I still had the most trouble. I'd been able to face the draft, face policemen wielding clubs, face the Hell's Angels when they rode their motorcycles through our peace march. So I wasn't exactly Mr. Milktoast in most situations. At work, I'd been seen as strong and honest, one of the few people who could consistently stand up for himself and others against the administration. But with the significant woman in my life, I still felt scared. Why couldn't I be as strong at home as I seemed to be everywhere else in the world?

It hadn't been that long since I wrote: "Well, you knew it all the time, the answer's in me. But when you're tired and all alone . . . would you go if someone smiled and said I'll give it to you if you'll give it to me?"

It was still true that when I was with Sheila, I merged with her. Our energy was so powerful I could lose myself.

Alone, I would ask myself, "Do I need to be a bachelor

longer before living with Sheila?"

I knew I didn't need to look around more to be sure she was the right one for me. That remained clear and strong. I would have liked some more sexual experiences with other women, but that would be possible with Sheila since she said she wanted a sexually open relationship and I thought I could probably handle that someday.

I did feel a desire to have more time to be free and irresponsible, to get up when I wanted, work or not work, leave my space messy. When Sheila and I were together, we were always working out some aspect of our relationship. I wanted time just to work out with me, not to be concerned with "she" or "we." Did I need time for more of that before living with Sheila? Could I get it while we were together?

I had a dream: Sheila and three of my friends and I planned a robbery, but I decided I didn't want to participate. I had a vision that we'd get caught, but I was afraid to tell the others for fear that they would be angry at me.

I told Brad and he seemed to understand. When I told Sheila she didn't seem disappointed at all, nor did she seem interested in finding out about my concerns. Instead she bubbled happily that it was all right if I didn't want to do it, and she had already arranged a replacement for me just in case I decided to drop out.

She went on adamantly about how nice he was. I felt madder and madder that I had been replaced in *advance.*

"His name is Victor Mature and he's so nice, very fatherly and nurturing," cooed Sheila.

"Did you fuck?" I asked with disgust.

Long pause, "No, but I wanted to," said Sheila, matter-of-factly.

"Why didn't you?" I asked.

"We were in the dorms and didn't want to get caught."

"Oh nice, a father figure that fucks," I answered with disdain.

Then I realized how accusatory I was sounding and said "I'm really just scared that something bad is going to happen and I'll lose you and all my friends, and I'll be alone." Sheila started to listen at that point and I woke up.

That was a powerful dream for me. At times, I did wonder what Sheila wanted from me. Did she really want a "father figure that fucks?"

After a week's vacation together in Canada, Sheila and I decided to move in together. Sheila's arguments were convincing — getting two places was too expensive and if we were going to be together, "let's do it." We found a two-bedroom house since we agreed that we both wanted to have a space of our own and two bedrooms would give us a chance to get away from each other.

From the day we moved in and Sheila began decorating the walls and I felt "well, this is going to be her place," the tension between us rose. I became more and more controlled and quiet and she became more and more critical and angry. Our fun times got fewer and farther between. But I kept thinking that any relationship that's worthwhile takes work. I didn't understand why, but it felt like I was completing something unfinished from my years with Lindy.

As the months passed by, I found I spent more and more time away from the house. I began to dread coming home. I wondered what we would be dealing with today. But then there were times when the clouds would seem to part and the love and excitement I felt when we first met would come through. I felt strong again and able to handle our hassles and still love. At those times, everything seemed worthwhile. All the fights and fears seemed to be leading us closer to a peaceful center where we could both relax. Then the clouds would close again, it seemed more quickly each time, and we were once again in the midst of struggling.

Jesus, I was getting tired of hassling — it seemed like all I'd been doing for the past five years. First with Lindy, now with Sheila. In my daydreams, I wanted to get away from it all.

"I want someone to be 'super-mommy' and make the world give me milk and honey. I don't want to look for a job. I don't want to see the kids. I don't want to work it out with Sheila. *I don't want to grow up.* Why can't I be Peter Pan? We keep thinking the issue is, do I want her, does she want me? I don't want to be single and I don't want to be married. I want to be mommied. And I have one just down the road. The pain and hurt I choose to feel gets me what? A view of myself as sick and helpless, which will eventually get in our way and split us up, which will give me an excuse to go home to Mommy. Lindy wouldn't play Mommy. My mom played it for awhile when Lindy and I split up, but quickly tired of the role. Sheila never would play. I can see the scene now. I'll be able to go home to Mom, 10 pounds underweight. We'll all agree that Sheila was a good, woman, but the timing just wasn't right. I needed more time to grow, to explore, to see who I am and what I want. Mom will sympathize and do my laundry and fix a few of her homecooked meals."

Yet we managed to stay together and I seemed to keep learning a lot about myself and things moved right along. I realized that a lot of our fights occurred when I'd agree to do something and then forget I had said I would do it. Sheila would get wild and I'd feel bewildered.

It seemed to be a pattern for me. When I was under stress I often agreed to do things that the other person (the woman) wanted me to do, then later I'd feel that I'd been tricked. Rather than renegotiate the agreement, I'd "forget" what the agreement was, or I wouldn't remember it the same way the other person did. That happened a lot with Lindy and was happening again with Sheila.

Releasing the Wild One

Sex had always been knotty for me. I thought I *should* like it and want it whenever I could get it, and a lot of the time I did. But it also was a center of anxiety and confusion for me. In spite of the fact that my first experience with masturbation ended in my knowing I'd "electrocuted myself," masturbation was still a great deal less complicated than trying to communicate with and please the new "liberated" woman. Sheila had instructed me since we first met about what she liked and what she didn't like sexually. At first I liked getting specific feedback instead of the vague groans and sighs that passed for communication from most women I had been with. But as we were together longer it seemed as if I was forever trying to get it right and the feedback felt more like criticism and blame.

This time it was an old littany with a new twist. "You don't really care about my feelings," Sheila admonished me. "I have to tell you again and again how to touch my clit so I get turned on. If you were a woman you would know what to do." I felt angry but kept my thoughts to myself. "What the fuck do you want? I'm *not* a woman. I'm a man doing the best he can." I tried to stay with her and hear her feelings and put mine aside for the moment. I thought I had done pretty well in hearing her feelings. But she said I hadn't done enough, I didn't really tune in and I hadn't shared my own feelings. By then I was feeling enraged, but it was all going inside. "You fucking bitch, you dump your fucking anger on me and I do my best to listen and understand what you are feeling and all you can say is 'you didn't listen good enough for me.' I feel like knocking your fucking head off." Another part of me was saying, "She's right, you don't really listen. You have to try harder.") I felt myself losing control. I yelled at her, *Let's get out of the bedroom and stop this!* Sheila screamed back, "I'll do it for you, but first I want to tell you how cold you've been to me." The rage and panic were building up in me. "I won't stay here and have you dump your shit on me," I screamed. As I turned to leave, Sheila spat out, "You coward." I turned and had the split-second image of knocking her through the window.

My head pounded and I couldn't see clearly. I knew I would explode if I didn't do something. The rage and the panic seemed to merge together and I knew I could end it by bashing her head.

Instead, I turned and smashed my hand into the wall. I knew I had broken it as soon as I did it. I felt a rush of feelings — pain from the blow, anger that I'd hurt myself, relief that I hadn't hit her, fear that my act of violence would drive her away, and underneath it all a vague feeling of power and delight.

I called my doctor, met him at his office. I kept fighting my desire to cry and say "I'm sorry." (That's what I used to do with my mother when I was younger, "I'll hurt myself, get sick, and then you'll be sorry.") Sheila was supportive and reassuring. The X-rays showed that I had badly smashed a number of bones in my right hand and my doctor recommended seeing an orthopedic surgeon. I felt proud that through the ordeal of seeing the doctor and getting the X-rays I hadn't been a "good strong man" like I usually was. I paced up and down. I didn't care if it upset other people. It made me feel better to cry and moan and I did that. I got pissed at the doctor because he was late. I picked a surgeon I knew and told the doctor I didn't care about "medical protocol" I wanted to talk to him myself. I saw the surgeon in his office by 11:00, was checked into the hospital, and had the surgery done by 2:00. The hand was put back together and four metal pins were put in the bones to hold them until they healed. I spent the night in the hospital and came home the next day.

When I got home I finally let out my anger toward Sheila for continuing to provoke and push after I said I'd had enough and wanted to stop. "You fucking bitch, you push and push and push. I can't get any space from you. I know why you've been beaten up by men before. You *fucking provoke* them until they blow up. You're goddamn lucky I didn't knock your goddamn head off." It felt good to let out some of my frustration and rage. I didn't know if Sheila really let any of it in, but it was good for me to let it out.

Everyone was very supportive after I hurt my hand. Steve came over for dinner, Mom came by for lunch. I was supposed to meet someone to discuss a new job at a teenage group home. I had finally acknowledged that my private practice wasn't bringing in enough money and the stress of never knowing how much I would make in a month was getting to me. I swallowed my pride and began looking for anything that would bring in some money. Working in a group home for delinquent boys wasn't my idea of the capstone of my career, but I was ready to take anything. My final interview was to be on the same day as my close encounter with the unmovable wall.

Now I was afraid I wouldn't get the job. Everything seemed bleak. I couldn't pay my child support, I couldn't take care of my family, I had no profession, and Sheila and I weren't doing well.

I remembered my father and messages I heard growing up. I knew I had failed my family and had failed myself. I felt lower than I had ever felt before. I remembered Sheil's gun that had been a source of contention between us ever since we first met.

She maintained that it was a violent world and she was going to protect herself. Her ex-husband had bought her the gun and taught her how to use it, and no one was going to take it away from her. I hated guns. They frightened the shit out of me. Their only use was to kill people and I was a lot more frightened of getting shot by Sheila during one of our wild rages than by some burglar. I also believed that fear and violent energy attracted more violence, and out of our desire to protect ourselves we drew to us the very energy we were trying to protect ourselves from.

We never did resolve the issue of the gun. It stayed hidden most of the time and I had almost forgotten about it. But I found it again and it held a new fascination to me. I thought how quickly all the confusion and pain could be ended. The thoughts scared me and I decided to get out of the house for a few days.

The day after I returned we had another blowup. It looked like I would get the job and Sheila was angry that we wouldn't have enough time together. I felt "there is no way to win with this woman." I blew up again, but this time hit the pillows while I screamed my rage. I let go of my anger, but was still careful not to hit anything with my right hand, which was still in a cast. My esteem was low. I needed to find some kind of center for my life. Women and work had always been the major forces in my life. When one was not working the other one always provided the stability I needed. Now I didn't have either and it was like not knowing who I was. I seemed to be stripping away the layers of my being as though I was peeling an onion. I wasn't sure what I would find inside. My hidden terror was that there would be nothing.

We celebrated our seventh-month anniversary together. It was a typical Jed and Sheila day, full of stress and love, beginning in the morning around snuggling. Sheila came into my room saying she wanted to snuggle. Her external posture was one of anger, which I'd learned by now covered fear. I was able to say, "Let me have two minutes to think about it." It took time to tune into what I wanted. I decided I didn't feel like snuggling. Sheila started to get angry, but we talked and we were able to keep things from escalating. Later Sheila said she was leaving, "I want to find a man who will give me the things I need. You're so fucking passive-aggressive I can never get anything from you. I don't want to live like that. I'm leaving." This time I could keep from feeling scared and panicky. I could call her on her behavior. "When you feel hurt you don't feel like you're getting what you want from me, and you threaten to leave and then cover me with your verbal abuse to cover your own hurt and justify your anger." To my surprise, instead of leading to a fight, Sheila seemed to appreciate my words and seemed calmer and less panicky. I didn't understand it, but out of some space deep within me was beginning to emerge a clear, strong source of energy and power. I had always gotten power from what I did. Now it seemed to be coming from somewhere else. I didn't understand it, but I liked the feeling.

I'd been feeling overwhelmed and pulled in all directions by people and things and it felt like too much. Instead of stuffing them, I began shouting them:

"Gene wants me to come to his school for a music program. Sandy wants attention from 'daddy'. Lindy wants support money, clean clothes, and clean children when they return to her. Leslie wants to be loved. Steve wants someone to talk to and be with him. Randy wants me to do a workshop for his group. Marlaina wants me to do a training program at Asilomar. Sheila wants me to 'get straight with us' and deal with her anger towards me. Joanne at U.C.

wants contracts and class schedules done. Every one of my clients want their own time and my personal touch. Jim wants to tell me how bad things are. Peter wants to tell me how good Jim is. My money-making side is afraid my whole private practice is about to fall apart. Ruthie wants to be held and hugged. The new house wants to get occupied. In this small town, even sitting alone, people come by and want to say hello. The couch wants to get sold, coins want to be appraised. Furniture wants to be bought. Sheila's furniture wants to be picked up. Brad wants friends to wish him well when he leaves. Seth wants company. *Fuck you all!*

At times I felt that my relationship with Sheila was just a continuation of my relationship with Lindy, as though I didn't finish the work I needed to do and now must continue on with that. Lindy and I went through the "image" layer of our relationship, woke up one morning and discovered there was a lot we didn't like about the "real person" we were beginning to see. We didn't go completely through the "negative" self we saw, but split up in the middle. It felt like Sheila and I were immersed in the fears of our being: my fear of being left, my nice-guy image — with hidden knives that get you when your back is turned — my confused "overwhelmed" state that protected me from hurt but kept me lonely, her fear of driving me away, her fear that she wasn't good enough, her demands that I prove myself to show I love her, her fear of my weakness and criticism. All these areas of our being were opening up for us to look at, and at times it was very turbulent and painful. But we were finding that below all the fears and hurts there was a positive core of realness that we were also contacting.

I felt like I was on a roller coaster. One day I was high and in love. Sheila seemed beautiful and our relationship perfect. The next day, I was frightened and depressed. Our relationship seemed to hold nothing but tension, and nothing in the world seemed to exist except our tangled web of love/hate.

God, the feelings were heavy. Sheila and I went to a show. She got so enraged with the girl for telling us the wrong time I thought she'd hit her. She yelled at the manager and as we began to drive away I had the strong impression that she was about to drive the car through the glass doors. At that moment, I felt she was quite capable of killing someone, and I was frightened.

That night I had a nightmare, similar to ones I used to have as a child. "It's coming at me, going to kill me. I can't run. I get back to my bed, but it stabs me in the back and I wake up screaming." Who was it? Where was the rage coming from? Sheila and I got into a fight before bed and the rage she expressed made me feel like she might try to kill me. She still carried the gun to protect herself against muggers. I wanted to run but couldn't. I wanted to strike out but I was afraid. She was getting too close. My stomach hurt. I was aware that as Sheila was yelling at me, I was hating her and wanting to slash the pillows apart with a knife. Below my rational exterior I felt murderous rage. I began to go deeper inside myself, through merky layers of violence and fear and strange fantasies.

"Mother violated my space. I had no space. She was always there. *Get the fuck away you bitch, or I'll kill you.*

"I'm sorry Mother, please. I didn't mean to be bad. Forgive me for hurting your feelings."

Mother was always nice. I can't get angry at Mother, she's nice.

"The bitch-witch will send you away like she did your father. She'll have you locked up like she did him."

"She'll get you at night while you're asleep . . . *The black witch will get you.*"

"I'll be safe if I get back to my bed. I'll be safe if I . . . . I want to kill her because I *hate* her. But she'll kill me first. If I don't *feel,* she won't know I hate her and she won't kill me. If I kill her, I'll die. *Trade feelings for life.*"

Tonight I saw Sheila's rage. I couldn't accept it. If she could kill others she could kill me. And I knew from my own panic I could kill her

We fought and I didn't kill her and Sheila didn't kill me. I raged and raged and *raged.*

I screamed for my *life.* "I was afraid you'd kill the people in the theatre and I was afraid I'd kill you." I was *alive*. My being wouldn't be destroyed and I wouldn't destroy her.

We went to Los Angeles the next weekend and attended a workshop with George Bach and Herb Goldberg, aptly titled "Creative Aggression — How to Fight Fair in Love and Marriage." It all made sense to me. It was natural in relationships to build up angry feelings, and our fear of "fighting" added to the pressure, until people finally did blow up and say and do things that were destructive. The strongest experience of the whole weekend for me was feeling angry at Sheila, going back into the room where the lecture had been, telling the instructor I wanted to try out the "Vesuvius" technique, and just letting it all out, screaming my anger and resentments to the walls. After three or four minutes of yelling I felt better, and I was complimented on how good a "Vesuvius" I had done. I didn't even have to talk to Sheila about it — just letting it out with all its fury helped.

At home we had a "Fair Fight Session" where we could each let out our feelings as loud as we wanted.

"You goddamn talk on and on and on," I said. "You never respect my limits when I've said I've had enough. You say the problem is all me and most of the time I'm so out of it I agree with you. You say you need time to yourself, but when I'm supportive of you doing that you accuse me of pushing you away. You continually push and provoke my anger. When I stop being a nice guy and let it out you say I frighten you."

"You're a goddamn jelly fish," Sheila jumped in with her eyes aglow. "You never want to deal with problems unless I initiate it. You're always running away. You say you want me but I don't believe it. You don't really care about anyone but yourself. I never know where you really are because you're totally dishonest. You hold things in until you blow up all over me. You're disgusting!"

After the "Fair Fight Session," I was exhausted but exhilarated. I had touched into a deep well-spring of powerful energy. I wasn't destructive, as I had feared, but clean and decisive.

Ever since I was a child I had been afraid to allow myself to experience my deeper Self. I knew that at the center of my being there lurked a terrible beast that would murder everyone I loved. I had spent much of my life trying to protect myself and my family from that destructive wild man. For the first time in my life I had gone that deeply into my being. I had gone to the home of the Wild One and was ready to kill him or die myself in trying. I would no longer live in terror.

What I found surprised me. I realized that the murderous rage did not come from the territory of the wild one, but lay outside it. When I confronted my own killer rage with Sheila, I found that at my core I would not kill. The rage came from fear, and when I went into it and through it, it began to disappear.

Robert Bly expressed this process of self-discovery very well in an article, "What Men Really Want." He described the 50's male — hard-working, responsible, and fairly well-disciplined. He didn't see women's souls very well, though he looked a lot at their bodies. The 50's male was vulnerable to collective opinion: if you were a man, you were supposed to like pro football, be aggressive, never cry, and always provide. But this image of the male lacked feminine flow, it lacked grace and compassion. It led directly to a view of the world that exploited the environment, used women, and easily justified fighting a war of "honor" in Viet Nam.

During the 60's, another sort of male appeared. The waste and anguish in Viet Nam began to force men to question the glorious image of the fighting hero. The women's movement challeged men to see women as equal human beings, and in the process encouraged men to explore their own feminine sides. I remembered the freedom of allowing myself to enjoy poetry, sunsets, and walks on the beach. I liked feeling support for rejecting war and the world of corporate exploitation.

Yet there was something missing. I felt "good" but I didn't feel "happy." Bly described us as "life-preserving, but not exactly life-giving." I realized that I had equated my own natural male energy with being macho, which meant for me exploiting women at home and destroying women and children at war. I knew I didn't want to be that kind of a male, and I didn't know there were other options than being macho and destructive or being gentle and soft. The strong women I met, women like Lindy and Sheila, seemed to like my gentleness. The male friends I knew seemed to be drawn to harder women and the women seemed drawn to softer men. It seemed to work out well for awhile.

I found I had become very good at understanding women, empathizing with their pain, valuing their goals as highly as my own, and satisfying them sexually, but I had a hard time saying what I wanted and sticking by it.

Bly helped me understand what was missing for me in his description of a fairy tale he had called "Iron John." As the story starts, something strange has been happening in a remote area of the forest near the king's castle: when hunters go into the area, they disappear and never come back. An unknown hunter comes to the castle, hears the stories, and sets off to solve the mystery. When his dog is snatched into a pond, he empties the pond little by little with a bucket. Lying at the bottom of the pond is a large man covered with hair the color of rusty iron. The hunter captures the hairy, powerful man and brings him back to the castle.

Bly explained that when the male looks deeply into his psyche he can see beyond his feminine side to the other side of the "deep pool." The ancient male he finds is covered with hair, which symbolized the instinctive, the sexual, the primitive, the powerful. This aspect of our maleness can be frightening. Once having struggled past my macho image, finding my deeper feminine energy, and enjoying the feeling of warmth and gentleness I had found, I wasn't anxious to leave that security to contact the wild, dark figure of "Iron John."

I had looked first for my feelings of wholeness to the macho male image, then to the strong women around me, and finally to the feminine within me. Yet now I was feeling a connection with a deeper energy. In Bly's story, this deeper energy was in the domain of the Iron John, the "deep masculine," the instinctive one who was underwater and who had been there forever.

In the story, getting in touch with this wholeness was not something gentle and nice. It involved going into the depths and confronting the dragons of death and destruction. It involved slaying the dragons of our fear in order to get to know the power of Iron John. This power was not the macho, destructive brute strength which I was afraid I'd find, but rather the power of forceful action, not without compassion, but with a clear resolve. As Bly said, when we talk with the hairy man, we are "not getting into a conversation about bliss or mind or spirit, or 'higher consciousness', but about something wet, dark, and low — what James Hillman would call 'soul'."

Reaching this deeper part of our being comes from a process of finally separating from our mothers' (and wives', girlfriends', and lovers') energy and reconnecting with our father. The psychologist Carl Jung made an interesting observation: he said that if a male is brought up mainly with the mother, he will take a feminine attitude toward his father. This was certainly true for me. I thought I was seeing my father as he was, but realized I was seeing him through the eyes of my mother, who saw men as weak and irresponsible. I had taken on that view of my father and hence of my own self. I realized I was beginning to discover for myself what my father was like and what it meant to be a man.

I realized that getting in touch with the "wild one" was true strength, the strength to shout and stand up for what I wanted. It did not mean moving back to the macho man of the 50's or giving up the feminine side of myself I had discovered in the 60's and 70's. As Robert Bly concluded, "Getting in touch with the wild man means religious life for a man in the broadest sense of the phrase."

I had a glimpse of the Wild One when Sheila and I fought, and again when I ran my first ever "Bay-to-Breakers" race in San Francisco.

I ran 7.6 miles from the Bay over the hills and down into

Golden Gate Park and up the Coast to the finish line in front of the old windmills along the dunes in the park. For me the race was one of those rare peak experiences that put me in touch with my power. The crowd of runners was huge, eight or ten thousand, of all ages and sexes, dressed in everything from tuxedos to the designer running shorts and gleaming bald heads of the Synanon women. I felt like part of a huge family, very much my own unique self, but an integral part of some huge organism. As the runners wound up the Hayes Street hill, a solid blanket of human color flowing down to the ocean, I felt like I was part of some huge social movement that would transform the planet into a better place for everyone.

I hit a spot going through Golden Gate Park where all thoughts and concerns of past and future disappeared. The tiredness in my body seemed to lift and float away. Everything seemed more beautiful, the colors of the park, the crowds lining the race route, the other runners, my own being. A deep sense of joy spread through me and I wanted to shout out my delight. I seemed to be going faster and faster as I flew past people who seemed to be standing still. It was as though we were all connected by invisible ribbons of delight, all a part of some huge kinetic sculpture. I flew across the finish line 93 minutes after I had begun. I felt transformed. It mattered not the least that thousands of people had finished in front of me. Walking back to meet my friends, I made a little bow to Iron John.

Chapter Seven

I Am One With Creation

Light Dispels Darkness /
Love Dispels Fear

We left to go on a trip, and didn't get 100 miles before we had one of our fights. We spent a day at Brad and Nancy's in Volcano, California, on our way out and got into a hassle there. I felt like I wanted to say fuck it and just forget the trip, but I didn't. We pulled out of Volcano with Sheila driving and me in the back waving goodbye to Brad. I felt like a little lost soul being kidnapped by the wicked witch. "How can I still feel so small and childish and powerless?"

I thought somehow that the trip would provide a change for us. I knew it would be a big change for me. When I went to Alaska I consciously cut myself off from women, friends, my mom and kids, and my secure surroundings, but at least I still had my work there. On this trip I was cutting off from all my ties, all the things that had provided meaning in my life, and instead of having a woman for support I had this angry harridan that was forever punishing me for this or that. Sometimes I felt I'd been cursed with the ability to see both sides of the question — and I always seemed to see her side more clearly than mine. The same issues were still there that we experienced at home: me hurting, not being assertive, expressing my hurt by being tentative. I saw Sheila as feeling hurt and uncared for, but expressing her feelings with hostility.

We continued our pattern on the road for the next two months. We moved along the highways with no destination, no timetable, and none of the traditional supports I had become reliant upon. Although we moved back and forth across America, the trip was really in the world of our interaction. The inside of the camper became our territory and the continuous fights became our world. Sheila complained and I bitched. I sulked and withdrew. Every day or two we had a major blow-up which would end in my deciding to leave and Sheila alternating with threats of reprisals if I did and loving touches if I stayed. Our trip continued on the wings of fear with love disappearing in the background. We moved deeper into the jungle of our own tangled feelings, and like *Apocolypse Now*, we moved toward disaster.

Having driven on whim for months, living in our metal cocoon, we crossed the Rockies a second time. We had our regular row and I retreated to the back of the camper while Sheila drove angrily around hairpin turns. Finally she demanded I come up front with her in a voice that chilled my soul. I refused and Sheila became livid. She demanded and I refused. She swerved even closer to the steep drop on the right and I realized she was planning to kill us. I knew I could stop her if I would do as she said and come up and be with her. But I knew I wouldn't go. I had spent too much of my life acting strong and feeling weak, knowing that ultimately women had some malevolent power that would finally destroy me if I didn't do what they said. I was tired of running and I was prepared to die and I knew that Sheila in her rage and fear was quite capable of driving us to our death.

I felt strangely calm. The fear disappeared and I knew I was free. I felt a kind of love for myself and Sheila that I had never felt before. Suddenly, Sheila swerved over to the side of the road and slammed on the parking brake and began to cry. I held her and comforted her. It felt like a spell had been lifted and a new light had entered our lives. When we camped that night we made love beautifully and felt close for the first time in a long while. We talked about being together.

I felt like we were seeing each other as we really were — not so much in terms of image — and we were seeing a lot we didn't like. We'd gone beyond the external positives that we saw when we first met: seeing her as sexy, assured, interested in growth and well-being, successful, liking children, enjoying movies, snuggling at home, being honest; she seeing me as strong, successful, articulate, sexy, open with my feelings, gentle, nurturing, sensitive, funny. But now we were seeing the darker side of each other and ourselves. It scared us. She was seeing me as selfish, frightened of being alone, unassertive, dishonest, irresponsible; I was seeing her as critical, blaming, demanding, frightened of closeness, vindictive, destructive.

As we continued our journey, my meditations kept leading me to a desire to settle down and stay put for awhile. I was hungry for some stability in my life, if only to see the same campsite for more than a day or two. Sheila wanted to continue East. An explosion seemed to come out of nowhere, a product of our collective frustrations and desires. Sheila said something. I yelled something back. Sheila slapped me. I slammed on the brakes and drove the camper into the curb. Sheila hit me. I hit her back. I got out of the camper, slammed the door so hard the window broke, and Sheila drove off.

I sat and waited for her to come back, which she always had in the past. But after an hour I thought, well this is it. We'd finally pushed things past the breaking point. Here I was on the streets of Greenbay, Wisconsin, with no money and only the clothes on my back. I finally started walking away, somewhat shaken, but feeling oddly free and light. I went into a health-food store, struck up a conversation with one of the guys who worked there, and after telling my story to him, he offered to let me stay with him.

Sheila called after seeing a note I left on the tree near where we had last fought. We agreed that she should continue on to New England and we'd meet in Florida in a month. We made arrangements for her to leave my clothes and money which sounded like something out of a James Bond movie. I had to first send her the money to pay for the window and sign over the traveler's checks that were in my name. Then she would tell me where she had left my clothes. When these arrangements were made, I found out that she'd taken them to a Catholic Church — shades of her former status as a nun.

After a day in Greenbay I decided I wanted to go immediately to Florida. Once on the bus, I realized that I wanted to make contact with my family, with my father's relatives that I hadn't seen in so many years. I felt some sense of wanting to know more about him, what his life had been like when he was growing up.

I hadn't seen my Dad for over 10 years. The last time we met was following my graduation from college, and he had disowned me when I wouldn't stay the summer with him and went instead to Mexico. At the time I acted angry. Underneath I felt hurt and guilty that I had not been a better son. I hadn't ever realized how much I had missed him since he left when I was three. Now, at age 36, I found myself crying as the bus drove towards Jacksonville, where he'd grown up and where his sister still lived.

Learning to Love

I hadn't seen my aunt and uncle since I was 14. They seemed happy to see me, though surprised at my call from Atlanta saying I was on my way and asking if I could stay. I got a job as a waiter at a fancy luncheon restaurant which doubled as a gay disco at night. (They warned me when I was hired so I wouldn't inadvertantly stop in for an evening cocktail and be shocked. I did stop in and rather enjoyed the atmosphere of the gay nightlife. It was much gentler than I had expected and I wasn't as afraid as I thought I'd be, though I went with my crazy cousin Charlie who I thought could protect me from "them" just in case.)

In the evenings, I spent hours asking about my father. I loved a story they told me about catsup. My Aunt Hattie had visited my mother and father in New York shortly after they had been married. My mother had gone to great lengths to make a beautiful casserole, with salad and all the trimmings they could afford during the Depression. When they sat down my Dad discovered that they had run out of

134

catsup. He sulked and nibbled at the casserole. My Mom jumped up, put on her imitation fur coat that I remembered snuggling so much as a child, and went out in the snow to find a bottle of Heinz. I had loved catsup as far back as I could remember. I put it on everything and told everyone I knew that I wanted to be buried in a catsup bottle when I died. I also recognized in the story the same expectations — that the woman should take care of a man's needs — that I had such a difficult time ridding myself of.

I got a card from Sheila, who had been staying with her sister in Philadelphia. They had always been close through the years and Sheila seemed to need the grounding of "family" just as much as I did. She mentioned in her letter that she had met a man, a friend of the family, and had spent some enjoyable times talking, mostly about us, she said. I had been missing her; the time and distance seemed to smooth over the conflict and I wanted her — to feel her touch. Something in her letter disturbed me and I knew it was the "man" and my fear that she would get involved sexually. Just the thought of her with someone else disoriented me. I finally called her. She said she was not ready to meet me and my fears of her being involved sexually were groundless. I still felt uneasy, but reassured. Whatever else were Sheila's faults, she was totally honest, and I settled down to a steady life with my family.

Three weeks later Sheila arrived unexpectedly from Philadelphia. Our first night together was like old times. She was gentle and loving and I felt strong and powerful. As we talked later I found she was depressed, more down than I'd ever seen her. She and her sister had had a fight and her sister literally threw her out of the house and said she didn't want to see her again.

The way Sheila told the story, it sounded like she was being the kind of hostile, critical, bitchy person she had been so often with me, and her sister didn't want to take it. Sheila seemed totally bewildered but somehow I felt vindicated. I wasn't the only one who had been the recipient of Sheila's acid manner. It broke the bubble of the illusion that I seemed so easily trapped in, feeling that it was all me and

Sheila was just an innocent bystander. I was always the bad guy. There was a part of me that just wanted to say, "It serves you right. Maybe now you'll start to learn what your way of being in the world is doing to people you say you love and care about." There was another part of me that wanted to take care of her, nurse her through her pain, but it was hard to do even when I felt like it. Her hurt turned so easily to anger and I always seemed to be the target.

The energy and power I felt seemed to melt away and I soon felt as lonely and hurt as I had been most of the trip. Nevertheless, we agreed to continue our odyssey together. I didn't know where I would find the peace to keep going but I was game to try.

The night before we were set to leave, Sheila threw another wrench into the proceedings. She told me she *had* been sexual with the guy she met in Philadelphia. I had to stifle my rage and frustration just to listen to her. She said she had no regrets, that it felt like the right thing to do at the time. She was missing me and felt that my invitation to come back early to Florida would have caused her to "give up on herself," so being sexual was a way for her to assert being herself. What with the trauma of her sister throwing her out and her feeling that she was at the very bottom of her being, she felt it was only fair to tell me now before we went on the trip so that I could decide if I wanted to continue with her. She said she wanted me to come, but that she needed total nurturing, no matter what she put out to me. She wasn't hearing my feelings, my hurts, anger, or rage, but needed me to be there for her totally, with a kind of unconditional love, no matter what she did.

I couldn't believe what I was hearing. I felt my blood beginning to boil. "Why the fuck should I be there for you after all of this? You treat me like shit the first part of the trip. You go to Philadelphia where you act the same way towards your sister who throws you out, and in the meantime you're off fucking some guy so you won't 'sell yourself out'. Now all you want is total love and acceptance, not for two minutes or two hours, but for the next month of this trip, and what you're offering in return is more of the same kind of shit. You must be out of your fucking mind to think I'd go for that!"

I stayed up all night thinking about it and by morning I had softened. I couldn't understand it — maybe it was the way she asked, so outrageously direct. Or maybe it was the challenge. By noon we were back on the road.

Things didn't change very much from the earlier part of the trip. Sheila continued to act the way she had, but something was different for me. No matter what she did or said to me, no matter how she treated me, I tried to be caring towards her. It didn't take long to realize that I'd never done anything like that before. I would be nice and caring with someone, but if they were rotten I eventually would treat them poorly or just get away from them. I found my new task incredibly difficult.

I found I could focus my loving attention on Sheila for awhile but then would get involved with my own hurts and pain and want to fight back or withdraw. At one of our stops I bought some books: one on religion, one on death and dying, and one on Zen Buddhism. If I was going to make this last part of our trip without blowing it or going crazy, I needed some help. As I began reading, I realized that it was my ego, the "me first" part of myself, that kept cutting me off and keeping my love from flowing.

When I felt hurt that I wasn't getting what I wanted I began to sense more and more that my selfish, childish ego and fear "I'll do anything if you'll promise not to leave" had caused me and others a lot of pain in my life. Somehow the last part of this trip, which had started as a gift to Sheila, was turning out to be an incredible learning experience for me.

The book on religion said that at every moment we can add a grain to Ego, Selfishness, Cut-offness, Me-Against-Them, or to Wholeness, Melting, Loving, Giving. I saw that my struggle to win over death by being somebody unique, by taking care of Me, by being strong was the illusion that Zen talked about. I began to suspect we actually win over death by going beyond ego, letting go of logic, and learning how to love.

I felt like I was a Zen student and part of my study was learning how to love, how to go beyond ego on this trip. I realized that I'd thought of myself as a loving person. But now I could see that so much of what I'd called love had really just been a game of "I'll give it to you if you give it to me." I'd never really known the kind of love that just gives. I wanted to keep going, keep trying to love unconditionally even when I felt hurt and scared and tired and needy. I wondered if there was a connection between my not really loving others unconditionally and my inability to really love myself in the same way. I'd been forever trying to prove myself and I wanted to love myself, but never felt deep inside that I was really lovable.

The Zen students I read about were often reminded that death is always possible, and there may be little time, so push on, live life, sleep it, eat it, drink it.

I wanted to do that in loving Sheila, to really commit myself to a full kind of giving. It seemed to take that for me. I needed constant reminders to keep to the task, to let go of my separate, private ego. It was so different than feeling like the perpetual victim. When I let go of ego, I let go of fear. I let go of needing to get, of trying to manipulate. Instead of giving myself away I gave to my self and my self grew as my scared ego diminished.

I was able to be loving most of the time, but the old fears still got in my way. My ego came to the fore and I forgot my vow to love Sheila. Fears arose, fear of Sheila going off with someone else, fear that I was loving to the best of my ability and it was too puny and short-lived. I wanted to run away. At times I wondered if I had enough love to really give another human being. Sometimes I gave all I had and Sheila acted like it was nothing.

As we continued driving west, I was learning I *could* love and give, even when the other person didn't give back love but resisted and gave back fear and hostility. It was possible to put my ego aside and tune into Sheila. I really couldn't lose my self, only my scared, anxious ego. I was getting ready to return to California. I felt stronger. I'd moved away from the terror in Jacksonville, wondering "where will I ever get the strength, the input of being loved, to survive the rest of the trip, much less give anything to Sheila?" Somehow out of my terror and fear, I found the strength I thought I never had. In learning to love Sheila, I somehow learned to love myself, somehow saw that there wasn't any difference. I went with trust and I found it was all there. I also got love from Sheila when I didn't demand it. I knew I didn't *need* Sheila in the way that I'd always needed women. By giving to her I realized my own strength. That six-month trip was a trip for me from fear to love. I felt it was just beginning, but it was there.

On the road, near the Ozarks, I did a meditation on ego. The message I got was: "The essence of ego is *isolation*. We see our self as separate. This sense of separation leads to *fear* and selfishness. I'm different from you and I must protect myself.

"*Death* is the basic fear because we see it cutting us off from all worldly ties, the ultimate isolation. For some cultures, it has meant the ultimate *union* with God, and so it is not fearful. But most modern people have lost that connection and feel afraid most of the time.

"The antidote for isolation is *enlightment,* getting out of our head, that part of us that categorizes and separates, and getting into our love being, that part of us that knows our true connections.

"We need a disciplined process for moving toward enlightment. An anti-ego, pro-self program. I've always been seeking something like that. Maybe Zen, maybe Aikido. The battle is inside, not out in the world where most of us think we are fighting."

On the road it all had seemed so clear. Back home again, it got fuzzier and our hurts and hassles continued. Yet something was different. I wasn't sure exactly what it was, but there was less fear. We stayed together for a year following the trip and when we did separate, with a great deal of respect and caring, we both knew that our relationship had actually ended with the trip. My old ego self would have said it was a failure. We couldn't seem to maintain our balance over time, and we'd slip back into our old ways. A deeper wisdom knew that it had all been perfect. I felt I'd gotten a glimpse of that wisdom, though it faded quickly away.

New Work /Hard Love

I had always tried to be creative at work, within the confines of a non-creative system. Life at work seemed to be a continuous battle to wring some degree of responsiveness and care out of a system that seemed to live with blinders on all the time. I had gone into "people work" because I knew business was "cut-throat" materialism and I was concerned about the human element. Ten years after graduate school I was beginning to feel I'd been fooled. When I began to look within for solutions to the problems of the work, I realized that I had enjoyed the conflict. I enjoyed being the angry young man who was intelligent and good at what he did, yet always at odds with the administration. It was an image I liked. I could say "fuck you" to my father who had left me and let me down, and at the same time I was trying to "help him do better." Going out on my own, I realized, had its own fears attached. Was I really the hot-shot I thought I was? Could I make a living on my own?

Yet I finally made the move and put together my own Center. I liked the title and the ring of authority even though it was just me being a private therapist, doing teaching, and consulting to a few agencies. And although things began slowly, I was making a living by myself. Even after doing it for two years I still felt I was "seeing if it would work." I saw too that whenever I doubted myself or my work I would find myself talking to a woman— either my mother, secretary, friend, or lover. They would invariably tell me what I wanted to hear, that I was talented, creative, and people wanted what I had to offer. They told me I was a success and I believed them.

But the doubt remained, the fears returned, and I would go again to ask for the "key." What they gave I finally saw was false hope. I took the potion they offered and never asked *myself* the hard questions. "Is this what I really want? How good am I? Am I really putting all of me into this work?"

I finally took the risk of asking myself. What I learned seemed true. I was open, honest, and I could share myself. I had a unique perspective on helping people and I was of value to others. I had a deep respect and caring for people and wanted them to realize their own power, not feel more dependent on me. The Center was a vehicle for me to make a living, explore with others my own ideas, and test out my own creative potential.

In Synanon, they used to talk about "hard love" and "soft love." "Soft love" was what most of us say we want, touching, nurturing, support, validation, hugs, kisses, etc. "Hard love" always teaches the lesson that "you don't need what you think I have, you've got it all inside you." It teaches that "I love you enough to give you the truth, to say 'no' when I don't want to do something, to hold back giving the immediate goody when you can get more in the long run the harder way." I got mostly hard love from Sheila and was able to use it rather than resist and reject it. I felt I could now apply both kinds of love to myself and my work.

Both my work and my personal life were much more integrated now than they had been. Working on my own gave me an opportunity to confront my fears and finally to do "people work" with much more joy and delight than I had ever thought possible.

Past Mommy and Daddy Fears

I decided I wanted to continue the process of releasing fears from the past and I found Ed Bourg, a therapist who specialized in bioenergetics. Although it scared me, I knew I wanted to do some work that would involve my body as well as my mind.

In the first session, we worked on me and my relationship with my mother, and my feelings that she didn't really want me. I tried to express my feelings to a chair, as if it were her, but found it difficult. I didn't want to "hurt her."

With some help I began to yell at her. "You were so god-damn frightened you smothered me with your love. Deep inside I think you were afraid you couldn't raise me and thought about getting rid of me, but you were so scared you couldn't even think of it. *I hate you for your dishonesty.*" Then I traded places and became her. "I *was* scared, but I loved you deeply, and although I had a times where I felt 'this is too much for me', I never considered, even in my deepest thoughts, giving you away. You always seemed with-drawn. I was afraid to reach out and touch you because I thought you'd reject me."

When I could really let go and get totally into each part, not holding part of me back because the other would be hurt, I could feel what it was like for "me" as well as for "her." I felt free. I realized I wanted to be touched more, but had held back because I felt too much touching would smother me. In the session, Ed held me and I cried and cried. I didn't have to be afraid. It was like reliving my childhood, but seeing it so much more clearly without all the hurts and fears.

In the second session, we worked on my feelings that I was the cause of my father's illness. I had thought that my birth interfered with his life, that the responsiblity of hav-ing a child was the thing that drove him crazy, and I was to blame. "Let me be, damn it. *Get off me,*" I screamed as I laid on the floor "being" my father. Ed pressed down on my chest. I could feel his pressures and knew that they had little to do with the little baby that had just come into the world. I knew for the first time that the baby was a joy to him and one of the few pleasures in his life at that time.

As I "breathed" myself back into childhood, I suddenly had the impression I was at the bottom of a huge amphithe-ater surrounded by adults who looked down at me. I was told that I was in this life on a provisional basis *only* and if I were to be allowed to stay I had to prove myself. I looked up and screamed, "I'll do anything, just let me stay." "*Do it,*" they said. "Just tell me what to do and I'll do whatever you say." Their only reply was, "Do it." I realized I had led my whole life in response to that "dream." I'd go faster and faster trying to prove I was worthy to stay alive, but never sure what "it" was I needed to do. In that session with Ed I began as a child and experienced myself getting older and older, all the time recalling instances of strength and love-ability. At the end I felt clean and strong.

During four other sessions, I found key experiences that had formed the basis for so much of my later life. Each time I re-entered the world I was able to integrate the experience in a way that let me feel more integrated and whole.

I Too Create Life /Coming Home to My Children

Having children always seemed part of the plan. I never thought about it very much, knowing I would go to college, get married, and have two children. We waited the appropriate time before having Gene and had always planned to adopt a girl if we had a boy. Adopting Sandy rounded out our family dream and we settled down to live our lives. I went to work. Lindy took care of the children. I prided myself at being more involved than most fathers and never had a glimpse of what real involvement was until Lindy and I were separated and the children were living with me part-time and we talked about them living full-time with me.

There was a world of difference between kissing them goodbye in the morning, reading them a story at night, taking them to the park on a weekend, and living with them 24-hours-a-day. I discovered the joys of breaking up fights late at night, dealing with ear aches that wouldn't go away, making breakfast and lunch while trying to comb her hair and find his tennis shoes, and worrying about how I'd explain being late to work again. I also discovered the joys of warm hugs and hearing "have a nice day, Daddy," when I'd take Sandy to school on my bicycle. I found the enjoyment of afternoon baseball when Gene wanted to play, instead of when I had the time.

I had known some of this in the eight years we shared the children, but I was so wrapped up in my work that the memories seemed to fade in a mist. I remembered going through the childbirth experience when Gene was born, helping Lindy with the Lamaze breathing. I cried for joy when he appeared in the world and I could hold him. I remembered the long nights getting up with Sandy, who never slept through the night her first year, and the peace I felt when I rocked her to sleep.

But mostly I remembered the children as being an intrusion on my time with Lindy and making noise when I had work to do, or whining and crying about some kid thing that seemed of no importance to me.

Everything changed with the divorce. I had them much more than I wanted them and I sometimes wondered if I could get through another night of hassling. When they were with Lindy I missed them and wanted them with me more, but I despaired at having to negotiate for time with my own children.

I'd get used to living a single life, having my own space, and then the children would arrive for the summer. I'd be ecstatic to see them one moment, then angry that my space had been invaded the next. Through it all we began to get to know each other in a much deeper way than I had known them before.

When Lindy said she wanted me to have the children full-time, my initial fear turned into excitement. I talked with friends and family and decided I would like having the children full-time. I had been with them enough to have some idea of what I was getting into, but I felt I was ready to make the plunge. I knew that for me, being one adult with two children was a pain in the ass no matter how well things were planned, and I began to explore ways of linking up with other adults to share childrearing so the kids would have other adults to talk to and play with. I understood what single parents meant when they said they began to talk baby talk after being with young children so constantly.

I remembered when Sandy went in for surgery on her cleft palate. She was so young, just a year old, and couldn't understand what was going on. Lindy and I took turns staying with her for the five days she was in the hospital. I would have hated to have gone through that alone and I was glad I had a partner to share the ordeal with. The doctors and nurses discouraged our presence, saying they were afraid we'd get in the way, but the hospital was such a cold and dismal place to be that we couldn't bear to leave Sandy there all alone. A chair beside her bed was all they would give us to sleep in, telling us with pasted-on smiles we were welcome to stay, but that Sandy would be well taken care of if we wanted to go home.

I remembered looking at Sandy through the night, so small and helpless, with splints on both arms to keep her from putting her fingers in her mouth and damaging the surgery. She seemed alternately in pain and terrified of the people in white who came most often to give her shots. I felt so helpless I cried along with her when they woke her up for the midnight needle.

There was always something special about my relationship with Sandy. On one level we always seemed to be getting into some kind of hassle. She was a real hellion and seemed to delight in disobeying me and pushing my limits until I blew up and wanted to cream her. I would get so enraged I would literally throw her into her bedroom, as much to protect her from what I felt like doing as it was to let out my own anger and frustration. Yet there was a real gentle bond between us too. She was alive and vibrant and definitely her own person. I liked her spirit and her power would often trigger my own, and I liked the feeling of rolling around together on the floor and acting wild and crazy. Gene loved to wrestle too, but he was always more subdued. He'd always check things out first, think about them before he'd decide how far he'd let himself go. In the summer he'd go cautiously into the pool, making sure he wouldn't go in over his head. Sandy would run and jump in wherever she happened to be and would go straight to the bottom of the pool. We learned to be constantly alert and would fish her out gasping and choking, only to have to rescue her again five minutes later. I felt a bit more sure that Gene would survive childhood.

For his fifth birthday, I took Gene to Disneyland. We flew down, just the two of us, and stayed in a motel across from the park. We never stopped talking the whole day. He seemed to be able to be an adult at will and discuss events of import and listen to my feelings, then shift to being a five-year-old and draw me right along with him. We ran through Bear Country and sang "It's a Small World After All," until we both fell into bed exhausted.

Shortly after Lindy and I separated, Gene and I went on a father-and-son backpacking trip with the YMCA. It was difficult, fatiguing at times, but it was a good chance for dads and sons to get to know each other, to struggle, to crab about how much we hurt, to play together. Gene was a delight, cheerful and self-reliant. He made friends with just about all the other kids and although he was generally off enjoying army games, Indians, etc., he would come for a kiss and snuggle every once in a while and we'd have a moment of contact.

The first night was unpleasant. I felt lonely, no warm woman to cuddle around the fire with. I remembered the family camping with Lindy the year before. But just as quickly as I remembered our snuggling, I remembered the fearful talks, wanting to be *the* person in her life, but afraid to say so, being tentative and fearful, wanting so badly to be loved and feeling that no one would really love me. Gene and I had one of those peak moments while we were lying together in our little pup tent after a hard day of hiking and playing. Gene asked me if we were going to get divorced. I said we were, feeling good that things were settled and everyone was handling their feelings so well. Gene got tears in his eyes and started to cry. When I asked what the matter was, he blurted out that if we were divorced, I wouldn't be his father anymore and we wouldn't ever see each other again. I started to cry too, and we both held each other tight and let our tears of love wash over each other. Afterward, I assured him that it was Lindy and I who were getting the divorce. He and I would always be related, I would always be his father, and we would continue to see each other.

After the divorce, things became so uncomfortable with Lindy and me that we'd drop the children off at my mother's house so we wouldn't have to see each other. We seemed to fight every time we met, so we worked out the intermediary to funnel the kids between us. It wasn't the best exchange point since my mom lived in a senior citizen's apartment complex and everyone was always worried about the kids making too much noise or bowling over a little old lady as they raced through the hallways.

On one such occasion, the kids got into it as soon as they got in the apartment. Sandy began teasing Gene and jumping up and down on the bed. As I usually did, I tried in my best fatherly, soothing voice to explain to her that jumping might disturb the neighbors. As she often did, she just looked at me and wouldn't respond. Usually her cold stare would get me angry and I'd be on her. But this time something was touched in me and I asked, "Is something going on inside you, Sandy?" I touched her leg and asked, "Aren't you feeling good about yourself?" She looked up, was very present for a moment, then burst into tears and threw her arms around my neck. We sat together, holding each other for a long while. Finally she smiled, then I smiled. No words were exchanged, but something very special had happened between us.

I found more and more often that when I'd try to do what I thought a good father would do, our interactions rarely turned out well. When I reached down from my human, here-and-now feelings and acted from that part of me, our interactions began to blossom. I felt it was such a gift to have these two children to learn from and grow with, even if it took me so many years to realize it.

Men Together

Oddly enough, my introduction to male liberation and men's consciousness came at a weekend workshop titled "Women in Transition." I had gone with my wife, ostensibly to better understand women's liberation and the process of change she was going through. On a more subtle level, I was looking for the same kind of support and understanding she was finding in the women's movement.

We gathered at Asilomar, a beautiful conference center on the ocean near Monterey, about 500 women and 20 men. The other men had been attracted as I was, I assume, by the small print on the brochure that encouraged male attendance. At first, it was a bit frightening to be in contact with so many women, and I wondered if my presence would be resented. I remembered some time ago going into a feminist bookstore with a woman friend of mine and being greeted by cold, icy stares from the women there, even though I was as interested in the literature as the women who were browing through the store. A little boy about eight, obviously the child of one of the women who worked there, also looked at me suspiciously. As I became engrossed reading books, I was only vaguely aware of him as he brushed by me in the aisle, until he so obviously tripped on my feet. I had to look up and notice his angry reaction to my presence. Later he finally brushed up to me and pushed a crumpled piece of paper in my hand. I almost cried when I opened it and read in his child's handwriting, "We don't like men here." What must he be learning about himself, I wondered, and felt a wave of love for our son Gene and the way we were bringing him up.

For the most part, the women at the conference seemed warm and supportive. The first evening we broke up into small groups and I found myself with Lindy and three other women. We quickly got into talking about why we were there together and our feelings about being a man and a woman. Before we were five minutes into our conversation, the leader cut in to tell us we were to be in groups with people of the same sex. I felt jolted, disappointed at first, but then remembered the reason I was here was to connect with other men who shared my consciousness. Surely the 20 men who would have the guts to come to a workshop with 500 women would have the courage to begin exploring their male identity. A group of five of us began to talk, I couldn't believe what I heard. The conversation began with sports and moved quickly to the foxy women that were all around and finally to a dirty joke that evolved from one man's being placed in a room with two women. I finally cut in and said this wasn't what I wanted to talk about. I could have this conversation, and had many times, in a locker room after a game. I wanted to talk about why we were here and what we were each feeling.

My words seemed to die as quickly as I uttered them and the conversation returned to its original level, though a bit more subdued. I wanted to scream, but just tuned out and half-listened. I felt the despair I had known so much in the past. I felt again like some kind of a freak, and very much alone. I thought if the men there were just like men at home, there just weren't any men who were searching for the things I was. I felt a real connection with the women there who bemoaned the fact that there weren't any good men at all "out there."

The next day, sitting in one of the workshop groups, I felt the presence of another man before I saw him. As the workshop progressed, we seemed to gravitate towards each other and at the break began to talk. He seemed to have the same concerns that I did and we both got tears in our eyes when I described my despair the night before. He was from Davis, California, and had started a men's group among fellow professors at the University a number of years before. His description of the experience and the sense of warmth that had developed made my mouth water. I couldn't wait to find a group like that.

Throughout the weekend, we seemed to keep running into each other. We met two other men, one from Los Angeles who had started a fathering group after his divorce, the other the husband of one of the women who had put on the conference. I felt a new sense of hope. If I had found a few who thought and felt the way I did, I knew there had to be others out there who had a similar attitude. They might still be few and far between, but at least I knew they existed and I wasn't totally alone.

Two months after I had returned home from the workshop I still hadn't found any signs of a group in my area, though I did hear about another weekend retreat in Santa Cruz with Dick and Marion Vittitow which was advertised as exploring male and female lifestyles and relationships.

About 20 people attended, and though the original plan had been to break into a men's group and women's group for part of the weekend, there weren't enough men to make that possible. I was disappointed, but valued the discussion and interaction with the few men who were there and with the other women.

We explored the ways male and female myths had permeated our views of male and female relationships. I realized for the first time how dependent on women I was for my definition of manhood. I had always looked to women to tell me how to act and what counted in being a man. I became aware too of how much the female myth had debilitated women and set up "the battle of the sexes." Men were angry at women for their insistence that we be as Gods. Women were angry at men for their God-like insistence that women be second-rate.

Somehow our true selves were inside all of that Male/Female garbage, strong and pure but sensitive and vulnerable. We needed to draw out that inner voice, but since it could be easily driven back with harsh words and actions, we needed to be gentle with each other as men and women.

I found in Dick Vittitow a kindred spirit who was able to articulate much of what I felt but had no words to convey. The weekend provided yet another ray of hope that I would find the kinds of supports I needed.

Two weeks later I ran into my friend Brad and found to my delight he was planning to begin a leaderless men's group with three or four friends and wanted me to join. I was overjoyed and couldn't wait for Thursday night for us to begin. We met at Brad's house in the country. Our group consisted of Brad's brother Rod, a struggling potter; Gary, a singer and out-of-work musician; Fred, a refrigeration repairman; Richard, a young rancher; Brad, my friend from college, a struggling artist; and myself.

I liked the fact that we had no designated leader and each person took responsibility for the direction of the group. I also liked that we weren't a "consciousness-raising" group, which for me had the air of trying to rid ourselves of our "sexism" so we could be more acceptable to liberated women. Our process was just to get to know each other and share whatever we wanted to in the most open and honest way we could.

The early groups focused on our relationships with women and the hassles we were generally having and the pain we were experiencing. It was nice to have friends I could be honest with and who were having the same kind of trouble I was. As we got to know each other better and began socializing and having pot-luck parties, we met the women we had all talked about in the groups. Later we laughed as we all agreed that they seemed a lot more enjoyable in person than the way we described them in our groups. Soon we began to talk about our jealousies and fears. Brad voiced a belief that most of us shared. "Regardless of how much we say we're friends, if there was ever a choice between getting involved with one of our women and keeping our friendship, I don't have any doubt that we'd each pick the woman."

We all agreed that we assumed that was true of the other men but believed our own friendships were more important than "scoring." Awhile later, Gary and I had a chance to test the theory. After Lindy and I separated, I felt lonely and horney most of the time. Gary had been dating Leslie, who I met at one of our parties. She and I had an obvious mutual attraction. I shared my feelings openly with Gary in the group, and though I acknowledged my attraction, I felt clear that my friendship with Gary was more important than getting started with Leslie. Over the next year, I felt numerous pressures to reverse my choice, but the friendship held.

Later still in the group's evolution, we began talking about each other and the feelings we had as we became closer. We talked about our homosexual fears and what we learned as kids that made any attraction to men a source of panic. We explored the different reactions we had to being touched by a man and the hunger most of us felt to be

151

touched more. We expressed our anger and learned we could be fierce with each other without it escalating to violence.

Throughout the group's life we learned how to trust each other and support each other as we dealt with divorce, relationships beginning, babies being born, jobs ending, fights with mates, and fights to find mates. For me, it was the first time I'd ever been able to be open with other men about my real feelings. I'd always found it easier to talk to women. They seemed more sensitive, more interested in ideas and feelings. My image of men was that they were harsh, aggressive, and shallow. It felt good to begin seeing and expressing another side of my being with men who were doing the same thing.

I remember with fondness the first time Brad really confronted me after we had returned from an evening where all the directors of growth programs had met. He pointed out that my telling people I was "the Director of the Center for Personal and Social Growth" was part of an image thing for me, and I was trying to make my one-person, private practice sound bigger and more important than it really was. I had to admit he was right. He said, "Hey, you don't need all the extra stuff. You're fine just the way you are, and what you're doing is fine, without having to make it sound bigger than it is." He broke my bubble and at the same time told me I didn't need it. I felt relieved.

I realized that saying Brad was "my best friend" was also an image — an image of what I would like, but a reality I was really afraid I wouldn't get. It was as though by saying it enough, I could make it come true. If I assumed it was true, I didn't have to confront the reality of where our relationship really was. I could see that I very much wanted Brad as my best friend. I'd never really had a "best" friend, and I found I still wanted that, a real buddy I could do things with and who knew me better than anyone and still loved me. It was scary to acknowledge that Brad and I weren't really that close, that though we'd known each other for 10 years and had been in the men's group together, there still was a distance between us and a reserve that prevented us from getting closer. Acknowledging what was true for us forced us to be honest about what we wanted in a friendship and what we were willing to do to bring that about. I had always seen my friendships as things that "just happened." I put a great deal of active time and energy into my love relationships, into my work, and into my children. I didn't think friendships needed energy — they would just grow by themselves and be there when you needed them. Looking back, I realized that most of my friendships had gradually faded away over time, even the ones that seemed important to keep. A once-a-year thread in the form of a card was usually all that was left of a once-vital relationship. In the fast-paced world I lived in, I never noticed the friendships slipping slowly away. Work and family occupied my time and it wasn't until my divorce that I realized how much I wanted to keep my few real friendships alive.

When I moved to the San Francisco Bay Area, I missed the weekly contact of my first men's group. The seeds of my next group, based in Marin county began with an experience of violence. Sheila and I were on our way to a party at the home of some friends of hers from the Zen Center in San Francisco.

I was feeling a little nervous, wondering how I was going to relate to these people who had become fellow students for Sheila but were still strangers to me. As we walked up the block, an approaching Zen student in a black robe stopped us and said, in a calm but very direct tone, "Be very careful, Chris Persig was just killed." Not much more was known. I felt shocked, a little sick, but not as frightened or panicky as I thought I would be under the circumstances. Sheila wanted to walk on, and go around the corner towards where it had happened. I had a moment of fear — I didn't want to be on the street with a killer lurking around somewhere — but I followed. At the next corner, the same corner where I got off the bus every evening, a body surrounded in blood was lying face-up at the edge of the street. Police were doing their work, taking pictures, checking pockets, etc. Zen students stood close by. Everyone was silent, but somehow very loving and peaceful. As I stood there I felt transfixed. A wash of feelings. "That could have been me lying there. How did it happen?" In that moment of being, I felt a connection with Chris, who I had never met. A young man, following a peaceful path, murdered senselessly on the streets of San Francisco. But there was no anger in what I felt, no fear, just that same feeling of "isness" I had felt on my past drug and non-drug "trips." This was death, this was real. I was there, I was alive.

Later that night I went to a Zen service held at the Center. I didn't understand the process and felt out of place among the black-robed Zen students, but I felt a part of all that had happened, part of the Zen Center, part of Chris, part of the night and the City and life and death.

At home later in our apartment, safe now from the streets, I did a meditation. "How do I make sense of this? Do I buy a gun, a knife, mace? What do I do?" In the meditation I got a clear image that Chris was killed because he was a "man." Something in his male upbringing contributed to his death. Maybe he didn't scream because men don't scream, or maybe he didn't run because only girls run, or maybe he was too nice, a reaction to being a man who was told we were all brutes. I didn't know how, but somehow this was the reality I was dealing with. In the meditation I also had a strong feeling that he was killed by a man, who had learned to be destructive. "Be strong, don't let anyone push you around, take what you need, love and compassion are for sissies." When I asked what was the best thing to do with all this, the answer I got was to learn to love better. I could protect myself and others by being more loving, by learning to give more love to the neighborhood, rather than buying a gun or a knife and giving more fear. I realized how much of my life had focused on rage and anger, either trying to hold it in or having it explode on my children or the women in my life. I saw myself lying dead on the sidewalk and also running away with a knife in my hand.

The experience with Chris had a profound effect on me. I wanted again to reach out to other men, to find other-ways of dealing with the violence we had all learned to use when pushed by our fears and failures. As if on cue I saw a poster describing a one-day workshop for men, featuring Herb Goldberg, the author of *The Hazards of Being Male*. The subject of the workshop was how to deal with anger.

The energy of 25 men meeting together for a day was wonderful. In one of the exercises, anyone who felt moved could stand up in front of the group and tell the "men" the ways in which men in our lives had let us down. The room seemed to catch fire as one man after another stood up, began with quiet measured tones, and ended with anger, rage, and eventually tears as we shared our hurts from unresponsive brothers and fathers and friends. There was a healing catharsis as we opened the wounds that we all carried from the men in our lives.

The following Thursday a few of us met to evaluate the workshop and see what we wanted to do in the future. Out of that gathering developed our Marin men's group: seven of us ranging in age from mid-twenties to mid-fifties with diverse backgrounds, drawn together by a common desire to get closer to each other and closer to what it meant to be a man. As with my first group, we evolved into a support group for each other, a point of stability in a flux of change. We explored many of the same issues, but issues took a back seat to the continued enjoyment of being and sharing.

We seemed to have fewer fears of being "male chauvinists" than we had before, and could have more fun just being who we were. In addition to learning about and honoring our feminine receptive sides, we could enjoy the rough masculine that we had all in the past repressed. We could make jokes about women and reveal our own sexism and laugh about it, without feeling we were terrible and needed our "consciousnesses raised." We could also have frank discussions about sex.

I loved the group meeting when we got very explicit

about what we did sexually with women. "You put it in where? . . . And then how did you move? When you say you started pumping fast, how fast do you mean? And when you push it in from behind, do you go all the way in or just part way, and what lubricant do you use, and did you really like it, and did she like it?" We all laughed, as much from the joy of sharing openly things that we never talked to anyone about as from experiencing sexuality with a new lightness of spirit.

We also developed rituals that increased our sense of being men together. We all loved the Superbowl and the excitement and energy that went with it. We began to meet early every year on Superbowl Sunday for a game of our own at the school near our house. The field seemed to always be wet and we had a ball slogging through the mud. We joked about inviting our women to be cheerleaders and to serve us beer and dance during half-time, but what we really wanted was to have them play ball with us. The game was more gentle than our childhood games, where someone would usually get hurt, and the competition was secondary to the experience of playing together. We also included children, who seemed to love this new kind of "macho" action.

Wet and a little sore, we would jam in front of the TV to watch the pros bash heads. We yelled and screamed and got high and generally revelled in our own male energy. It was fun to share it with the women and children and to feel their enjoyment of the male power we were all tuning into. We all realized we had lost something in our fear of being too masculine. We found we didn't have to be brutal to enjoy pushing up against each other and flexing our muscles.

Our group's anniversary became another ritual we all shared. We met for our third anniversary last year. We saw how the group had evolved and changed, how our relationships with each other had grown and deepened. The membership hadn't changed much over the years — one new member joined, and one dropped out.

Gradually, little by little, we'd been able to reach and

touch each other, to express the feelings we'd hidden so long, to move beyond our ego battles and needs to control. We shared our hurts, anger, loneliness, and frustration, as well as our excitement and joy, laughter, and love. We gave each other massages and we squared off against each other on the field. We helped repair each other's cars and we soaked in Tom's hot tub. We learned to be ourselves and we learned to be friends.

Chapter Eight

I Am A Man

Tasting Death

Mom called one Friday complaining of chest pains, and I took her to the hospital. She was OK, but the X-rays showed an aneurism which would have to be operated on. For the first time in my life, I had flashes of her dying, but I pushed them out of my mind. Someone in my men's group asked me what I was going to do when my mother died. My response was immediate and angry, "What do you mean? You're talking like she's going to die." "She is someday," Brad said. His words and the reality they contained seemed so strange and unreal. He might have been saying someday I'll flap my arms and soar into the sky. My intellect was quite comfortable with the knowledge that we all die sometime, but I couldn't handle the feelings that my parents would actually be included and that sometime could be tomorrow or next week.

I waited in the lobby during the operation, for the first time experiencing the reality that my mother might die. I knew from conversations with her that she was much more comfortable with the possibility of dying than I was. Her fear as an adult was that she wouldn't live to see me graduate from high school. She'd long ago passed that milestone and had lived the life she wanted to live. I admired her calm with a life well-lived. I read again the words of Elisabeth Kubler-Ross. They had much more meaning for me now. "When you love give it everything you have got. When you have reached your limit give it more and forget the pain of it because as you feel your death it is only the love you have given and received which will count and all the rest — the accomplishments, the struggles, the fights — will be forgotten in your reflection. If you have loved well then it will have been worth it, and the joy will last you until the end. But if you have not, death will always come too soon and be too terrible to face."*

I knew my mother had loved well in her life, though as she would acknowledge not always wisely. As they rolled her out of the operating room and told me she would be all right, I breathed a sigh of relief. I knew I was closer to accepting her death when the time came, but I was glad the time wasn't now.

In the weeks following her operation, I began to feel down. Life seemed so tenuous and uncertain. There didn't seem to be anything I could hang on to and rely upon. Mom would die someday. Marriages didn't last a lifetime. Sometimes I wondered whether I would ever have a relationship again that lasted more than two months. My career kept changing and sliding out from under me. My lifelong friends moved away and letters got fewer and farther between.

I began feeling cold and afraid and wanted to run to someone but there wasn't anyone I could run to. I wanted to make the feelings go away but they persisted. In desperation I decided to get into the feelings, to "hang out" with this deathly loneliness I felt. Gradually a feeling of well-being came over me. I felt peaceful and at home. It was the first time in my life that I'd experienced the peace of knowing I was totally alone in this world, and that was OK.

I remembered the same deathly cold feelings at times in my relationships with women. They'd creep in during times of silence between us. As the silence lasted I'd begin to feel panicky and would immediately say something, as if my words could provide a lifeline to my partner and forestall the cold death from getting a hold of me. I found a poem on an old scrap of paper. I hadn't the faintest idea who wrote it. It was on silence and it felt right for me now:

*Elisabeth Kubler Ross, *Living with Death and Dying,* 1981 MacMillan

I am afraid of your silence because of what it could mean. I suspect your silence of meaning you are getting bored or losing interest or making up your own mind about me without my guidance. I believe that as long as I keep you talking I can know what you are thinking.

But silence can also mean confidence. And mutual respect. Silence can mean live and let live: the appreciation that I am I and you are you. This silence is an affirmation that we are already together, as two people. Words can mean that I want to make you into a friend and silence can mean that I accept your already being one.

My Father /My Self

I went to a workshop in the Santa Cruz Mountains. Sitting alone by a stream, I felt the sunlight filter through the trees. I watched a bug flying about and I felt very warm and calm.

The stream bubbled and gurgled as I wrote in my journal. I felt my father's presence, as if he was sitting beside me and writing in his journal, approaching 40, wrestling with the same questions of survival and authenticity, what's good, what's worthwhile. He also felt the burden of making it, of proving himself. He also felt responsible for the family. I remembered as a little kid somehow knowing that he didn't "make it." He wasn't successful. He wasn't able to support his family. Somewhere before age six, I made a vow that it would never happen to me. I would survive and my family would always have enough. I would never turn out like my father. I started selling greeting cards when I was eight or nine and I'd been "making it" ever since. The anger and hatred, the fear that I'd turn out like him, had disappeared by now. As I approached 35 and found myself dealing with the same issues he dealt with, I felt like I knew him better, not as a child, but as a fellow adult man wrestling with the same ghosts and goblins.

The connections with my Dad through the years had always seemed confused and somewhat bizarre to me, but on that day his presence was very real and very gentle.

I remembered the confusion and pain I felt as a small child visiting him in the Mental Hospital, and the fear I felt when I was 12 and was told he had escaped. He never came to steal me away as my mother had feared, and through the years we wondered if he had died. He had definitely been an "absent father," but his influence on my life seemed profound without my even being aware of it. On the eve of my college graduation I got a note from my uncle in Florida saying they had "run into" Dad in Los Angeles living under an assumed name and surviving on the streets. They begged me to help him. It was like getting a message from another planet. When I walked across the stage at graduation, with my girlfriend, mother, and grandmother sitting proudly in the audience, I saw him disappear into the crowd. I knew it was him and I knew he was real, but nothing else about the whole situation was clear.

That summer I went to Los Angeles and found him. We agreed to meet at a coffee shop he knew. I was alternately excited and terrified at the thought of the meeting. I wanted to know my father and I was afraid at what I might learn. We talked non-stop for six hours. He told me in detail the horrors of the years he spent in the mental hospitals and his final escape. He described coming to Santa Monica and living out of garbage cans and gradually building a marginal life for himself along the beach. My first reaction was, "Jesus, my father's a bum." He went on and on about the hatred he felt for his brother and sisters and my mother for putting him in "the concentration camp," at times including me with the family he hated and at times saying that I was exempt. Then I thought, "It's even worse. He's a crazy bum."

Throughout the summer, I visited him in his small apartment along the beach. We walked along the boardwalk and he introduced me to all his friends, who seemed to be everyone we met — the local librarian, all the shopkeepers, waitresses, and even children. Everyone said what a fine man my father was and how proud I must be. He told me about the puppet shows he put on for the children, which had been the first way he had learned to communicate with real people on the "outside."

I began to see my father differently. I began to see a man with the courage and stamina to escape a prison, survive, not get caught, make a new life, develop friendships, and give something back to the community in which he lived. I could in truth say I felt proud of him. The pride turned to anger and fear as the summer drew to a close and I prepared to begin medical school in San Francisco. It started when he wanted to introduce me to all his friends and tell them the story of his long-lost son. Then he wanted to stop strangers on the street to tell them, and finally one day in a restaurant he stood up on a table and tried to get everyone's attention and tell them his story. I was embarrassed and didn't know what to do. As the day approached for me to leave, he began to get very sad, and begged me not to go. No reassurance about staying in touch and seeing each other seemed to help. Finally he got angry and began screaming at me, telling me I'd never make a good doctor if I wouldn't even take care of my own father. He said he was sorry I'd found him and never wanted to see me again. I felt a whirl of feelings as I fled his room for the last time. I was hurt and angry and confused. I didn't understand what I'd done wrong, but once again I knew I'd failed him.

The contacts over the next 15 years were strange. Once I saw him at a peace march in San Francisco. I knew he didn't see me and I walked on past. Years later I happened to see him doing his puppet show in Berkeley. Again I walked on past. I didn't want to be hurt again. One day on my way to work, I stopped to buy a *San Francisco Chronicle*. It felt odd to buy one since I got the paper at work, but I put my money in the machine, pulled out the paper and just about fell over when I turned the paper over and saw a half-page picture of my father on the front page. The caption read, "Tom Roberts, local street puppeteer, seen examining the art work for the Street Fair to be held . . . ."

There were no other "strange coincidences" during the next five years, yet I often thought about my father. I went to Florida and talked to my family about him and felt like I wanted to see him. I had no idea how to find him, but just felt that somehow it would happen. As my thoughts were repeatedly drawn to the past one day, I realized I had missed my bus from San Francisco to San Rafael and had to wait a half-hour for the next one. Two stops after I got on the bus, he got on, passed me without noticing and went to sit in the back. My heart was pounding as I thought, "Well this is it. Am I going to talk to him, or let it pass?" I changed seats and sat down beside him. He gave no sign of recognition that I was anything other than another passenger on the crowded bus. As we got closer to San Rafael I finally began talking to him, first about his puppets and then finally saying, "I'm your son," afraid he'd say "I don't know who you are. I've never seen you in my life." My heart skipped a beat when he answered in a low, gentle voice, "I know. How are you?" We stopped for coffee in San Rafael and talked again, but now there was a light in his voice. He seemed less angry and more open. He told me about his recent life and that he'd been living for five or six years in San Francisco, though he wouldn't tell me where. I told him about me and about my children. As we sat there this time, we had become more like equals, less afraid of rejection, but still father and son. I talked about some things I had written and he showed me some of his poetry.

He autographed a little two-page sampler of poetry he had written called Heart Beats and Pulse Beats. "December 12, 1979. Jed — Each one will find his own way to these fragments out of me — Peace, Tommy." One titled Resiliency spoke to me deeply about his life:

> Resiliency —
> One of human Kinds
> Finest graces —
> Time and time and time

Without end —
life bends us, twists us,
Knots us, stretches us,
Out-out-out-out
Till we're positive
We're going to break —
But out of our pains —
Our agonies —
Our heartaches —
We snap back and go on —
That power and strength
To be stretched and stretched
And stretched —
And then to snap back
Again and again and again
And go on
And live on —
Of all human Kinds
Finest graces —
One of the finest
Is
Resiliency

I gave him my address since he didn't want to tell me where he lived or when we might see each other again. It felt good to have been with him and I loved him deeply. A week later I got a postcard. "It was a very special coming together — Gave me renewed Hope — Have a good life — Peace, Tommy." I felt like we were going to keep contact and know each other for a long time.

That Christmas Eve, Sheila told me she wanted a separation. I wasn't surprised, but I was hurt and I left the house wanting someone I could talk with. I thought of my renewed family ties with my father and wished I had some way to contact him. I had a feeling he would understand about rejection, and besides it was Christmas Eve and I wanted to wish him well. He must have spent so many alone. Since I didn't know where he was I decided to go to the coffee shop where we had met and if nothing else just sit where we sat and remember our first meeting. I wasn't totally surprised when I walked in and found him sitting alone at a table.

As I approached, I realized something was different. He barely acknowledged me as I sat down and he seemed lost in thought. When he did talk it was as though our previous meeting had never occurred. He berated me for leaving him after college and for all the lonely Christmas Eves he had spent. This time I didn't run and hide. I told him I came to be with him and share our time together. I had even brought him a Christmas card with words of love and caring. I wasn't responsible for his past hurts, but we could care about each other now. He seemed to wrestle with my words, but finally returned to his anger and blame. Again I told him I wouldn't let him abuse me, that I wanted to share our connection, not his anger from the past. He couldn't seem to shake the past though, and finally screamed I wasn't his son and he wasn't my father, and told me to get out of his life. I felt his words go through me, but they just stung, they didn't wound me anymore. I told him he'd have to make peace with himself about his relationship with me, but as far as I was concerned he was my father and I was his son and always would be. He jumped up and left the restaurant. Ten minutes later, I left too with tears in my eyes, not so much for my own loss, but for his, for the needless anger he still carried, and for the lonely nights he would still live with. But as I walked I knew, from somewhere deep within me, that everything was as it should be. We each had to walk our own path in this life and his was no worse or better than mine.

All that remained for me from our time together, and all the time apart through the years, was a feeling of love and peace. I somehow knew I'd never see him again in this lifetime, and I thanked him again for being my father and wished him well.

Once again I began teaching a class on something I wanted to learn. I had long since found that we only teach what we need to learn and my class, "Men and Women: Exploring the Passages of Adulthood," was my way of exploring these issues.

I talked about Elizabeth Janeway's ideas from her book, *Man's World Woman's Place.* She explored the reasons why people cling so strongly to the belief that men and women are psychologically different and that men are destined to be out in the world, to dominate and make things happen, and women are destined to remain at home to take care of the house, the children, and her man. She concluded at the outset of the book that the "reality" cannot be gotten by stating "facts" to show that women are not now at home and never have been in the way that we often think, but that the idea was a myth and could only be understood by exploring the needs, wants, and expectations that support the myth. She explored the myths of female weakness, and found below it the myth of female power. I'd been saying for a long time that we wouldn't understand male/female relationships until we explored the reality that both men and women are born of a woman who in our early experience was all powerful. A man grows up to marry a woman who he is "supposed" to dominate, but who he is deeply dependent upon and frightened of losing. A woman marries a man she is "supposed" to be subservient to, but who she deeply feels superior to. Men are afraid of women's lib because it raises a fear that they had long repressed.

I shared with the class my feeling that the first step of my own liberation was to recognize and acknowledge my own fears and my dependency on women. It was only then that I could begin to assert my real strength, not the pseudo-strength of the macho man which was really based on fear.

During the class we did a "fishbowl" exercise in which the women sat in the center and talked about their experiences being women while the men sat silently around the outside and listened. As a man, I felt envious at the ease with which the women shared their feelings with each other and the way they opened up with real concerns and fears. Their sharing touched a place within me I was just beginning to recognize. When the women ended and we men began to move into the circle, one woman patted the place she had just vacated as if to say, "Here take my place and be comfortable." I nodded a thanks, sat down, then immediately moved. She patted the spot again and I moved back and sat there again. But then I moved again, and immediately burst into tears. This had all occurred in a period of 20 seconds as the "men's group" was forming.

Through my tears I finally was able to say what I was feeling. The invitation to "sit here" was one I responded to all my life. I knew that women had some magic power that I could perhaps get if I could get very close to them. It was as though I had always had a cord attached to me that I need to "plug into a woman" in order to get the power to live. In that moment of moving into the circle I knew I had been doing that all my life and that I couldn't do it any-more. I had to find my own place, my own source of power. My tears were for the joy of finally seeking my own power and for the fear that I wouldn't find it.

As we talked in the group most of the men could iden-tify with my feelings of seeking some kind of power from women. It was a power we associated with producing life, being loving, and caring about children and the world. We all felt we lacked, or had lost, some sense of that power and beauty. As we talked we all sensed that what had been lost could not be found by looking for it in women but if it were to be found at all, it would be by looking within.

Weeks later, I was lying in bed listening to a song by Kate Wolf called "Great Love of My Life," in which she sang wistfully to the special person who she had once loved. I began to cry, softly at first, then with great sobs. I thought about Sheila, Lindy, my mother, old girlfriends, even my first "love" when I was 11 years old. I seemed to be wailing for all the women in the world I had loved and lost, and for all the joy and pain I had felt. When I thought I had cried out all the tears I had inside me, it was as though the floor gave way and the depths of my tears increased ten-fold. I realized I was crying for the woman in me, for all the times I had pushed her aside to seek the next conquest, to find the next source of power. I cried for the betrayal I felt in denying her and I cried for the joy of knowing she had never left. I had finally come to know the Great Love of My Life.

Weeks later when one of the men in my group suggested we go to a "Rajneesh Chaotic Meditation," I was still feeling the glow of my "female half." I felt as though I worked out about six months' or six years' worth of feelings within the hour period of the "meditation." I didn't understand many of the symbols involved, but basically we worked in a group. As it turned out, the men's group all attended together, and since there was only one other person and the "guide," we had the place pretty much to ourselves. The meditation was divided into 15-minute sections. We were given blindfolds so we wouldn't be hampered by seeing what the others were doing. It was a good thing, too, since what we were doing must have looked weird. The first 15 minutes were devoted to jumping and moving in time to music, then towards the end of the segment, we were told to raise our arms and keep going. The guide kept us from bumping into the walls or into each other. In the second segment, we continued moving and making whatever sounds we wanted. In the third 15-minute period, we were encouraged to express whatever emotions we wanted, crying, screaming, whatever. The final 15 minutes was a quiet, restful period. During the hour, through a combination of the exhaustion of jumping around, and laughing, crying, yelling, and screaming, I went through my whole experience of being with Sheila and Lindy and my Mom. I first felt restrained, cut off from my feelings, just going through the motions. Then I got angry and let out what seemed to be years of pent-up anger. That subsided and turned into hurt and sobs as I rolled on the floor. I had a visual image of turning away from Sheila and all women, and turning toward the other men in my life, and finally an image of being all alone, but not lonely. Finally, I had another image of joining hands with Sheila on one side and Lindy on the other, and dancing together with joy. As the meditation ended, I felt peaceful and more whole.

Reflecting on these experiences later, I began to realize that my life had been a journey toward wholeness. To feel complete was a process of becoming aware of the ying and yang, the female and male within me, instead of looking for completion from someone else. The intimate relationships in my life and my "problems" with women were really a reflection of the degree to which I was able to balance the male/female energies within myself.

My conflict with Lindy, my resentment of her for being free and acting on her new-found power, was created by my inability to act on my own power. I created criticism and judgment from Sheila because she reflected my own inner judgments of myself. As I began to reconnect with my own feminine flow and to use my male energy to back up and support my intuition, I had less and less need to keep trying to get those needs met through intimate relationships in my life.

My Own Spiritual Practice

Unsure of what I wanted to do "professionally" after 12 years as a therapist and teacher, I decided to get a job as a waiter. Howard Johnson's in Mill Valley was taking applications and I put down that I had had some experience in Florida as a waiter. I didn't put down that I had a master's degree in social work, and I was hired on the spot. I had always thought I needed a prestigious job, complete with title, in order to feel good about myself and feel useful. Now I was doing "menial" labor, getting minimum wage plus tips, and loving it. I found I could enjoy working with young people who had no ambition but to get loaded and get laid, and I could enjoy the people work of serving others, rather than getting paid by someone to "be professional" and fix their lives. I stayed for a year.

I still had a difficult time, though, when I signed up for an Aikido class and had to write down my profession. At first I wrote teacher/therapist/waiter. I later got a new card and just wrote waiter.

I had been drawn to Aikido for a number of years, ever since I had seen a demonstration of various martial arts and felt the gentle power of Aikido. I'd found lately in my life a new way of seeing potential conflict. Since being with Sheila, I had learned to see conflicting energy as a gift for my own growth, rather than something to run away from or fight. Aikido teaches us to protect ourselves *and* the attacker through merging with the attacker's energy, and now I was ready to learn how. Although it all felt new and a little scary, I was excited the first time I worked out on the mat.

I continued going to Aikido, even though I felt sick and dizzy at first. Soon I began to enjoy the strikes and falls, the blending and interacting. I also liked the physical discipline and the awareness of my body that it brought me. I began to see the effects in my life outside the practice hall, especially in crises and under stress, when I found I had learned to "stay home," feel my depth, and let my energy extend out.

I read in a book by Suzuki Roshi that we in the West had inherited a dualistic tradition from our Hebraic and Greek past, including an irrationally nagging conscience from the Hebrews and an excessively dividing rational mind from the Greeks. That certainly applied to me, at least. Aikido helped me continue to unify my being and to become flexibly strong without being hurtful. It helped me let go of my super-critical self, and not rely so heavily on my rational mind. When someone in the class was moving in with an attack there wasn't time to wonder which hand goes where or which direction to move. I just did it. Aikido also teaches that whatever conflict we experience in the world is a reflection of our own internal conflict.

We had a "Samurai War," one of the most exciting experiences I'd had since beginning "Energy Awareness" classes — a "non-throwing" extension of Aikido. In a simulation of what it would be like living in Japan as a Samurai in the time of *Shogun*, we got a chance to experience ourselves in an environment where there was no such thing as democracy, where every action was at the discretion of the ruling Liege lord, where death could come in an instant, and where we practiced living with courage and respect for the Way of the Warrior.

Beginning the game, I was ready to experience the excitement of battle and really get into the whole process. Two minutes into the "War," I was dead on the battlefield, having died in my first battle instantly, as a result of losing "paper-rock-and-scissors," a simulation of a sword fight. In that moment, I got a glimpse of what death was like. In an instant, all my concerns about my job, my future, my children disappeared. Everything was now, and it all ended in an instant. No more fear or pain or hurt. I felt free.

As I lay in the "burial ground" waiting for the War to end and for the dead to be "resurrected," I had an image of talking to my grandmother, who had died many years ago. We "talked" about what it was like being dead, and laughed about how we were able to still talk to each other even though our bodies had died. Then I saw my father coming up. I asked, "Are you dead, too?" He smiled and said he was. He looked young, the way I remembered him when he carried me on his shoulders in the park when I was three. I had never believed in anything after death, but this felt like it was in some way real. I could talk to the dead. Their spirits were still here and very real. It also felt like this was just a game that I was making up.

Following Aikido practice one day, I attended an event called "Miracle Singing." I couldn't believe I actually went to something called Miracle Singing. If I hadn't been lonely, with nothing else to do, and if a friend named Marcie hadn't called to invite me, I never would have gone. I'd always hated anything resembling syrupy religious stuff — people being one in Jesus, "Save the poor sinner, let's all give a big hug for the lord, Hallelulah!" What I found was quite different than I had expected. People sat around in a big circle and sang songs that were simple and easy to learn, with guitar accompaniment from a tall, gentle man named Maitreya Stillwater. Below the syrup there just seemed a lot of gentle love and caring, and besides, I had always been a sucker for good folk music.

Later that week, on my way to a job interview, I felt drawn to stop in a bookstore. I didn't know what I was looking for, so I just casually browed around. As I was getting ready to leave I caught a few fragments of conversation between a customer and the woman behind the register. They were talking about a book by a local author, Dr. Gerald Jampolsky, who I learned from eavesdropping was a doctor who had been working with children, many of whom were dying, helping the children and the families deal with the reality of their lives ending. The book they were talking about, *Love is Letting Go of Fear*, intrigued me. The title sounded very much like an idea from the TORI group; they said that there were only two basic emotions, fear and trust, and we always have a choice of which emotion to experience. I picked up a copy and thumbed through the pages. I caught a glimpse of the words "Course in Miracles." I thought, oh, shit, here's some more of that religious stuff, but then remembered that they'd mentioned something about the Course in Miracles at the Miracle Singing. Since I didn't believe there were any coincidences in life, I decided I should buy the book.

When I read the introduction, I felt he was speaking for me and to me. Jampolsky is an intellectual, a no nonsense psychiatrist in the business of helping people, but he was never quite comfortable with his own life, always searching for something, but rejecting religion as being anti-intellectual and mushy. He found something called "A Course in Miracles," and it changed his way of living and looking at himself and the world. I definitely saw myself as an intellectual searcher, who was beginning to find some kind of spiritual connection that was making my life more whole and meaningful. Maybe this was another step in that process for me.

In reading Jampolsky's book, a great deal of what he wrote fit for me in terms of my relationships with women. When I thought I needed love from some other person outside, I became manipulative: "I'll give you love if you give it to me." I ended up "loving" the person who gave me what I wanted and "hating" the person who wouldn't. Somehow my relationship with Sheila taught me that to love in that way wasn't really love at all. It was actually a trap. We could never get enough from outside, so we always felt frightened, either fighting to get more or trying to protect what we had. What I got from reading Jampolsky's book seemed to unify much of what I knew about the "spiritual" side of my own life.

I started to feel I was learning, slowly but surely, to be healed, and to be calm, happy, centered, and peaceful in relationships with others. To "be healed" means letting go of our illusions of separation and returning to the oneness of Creation. We can do that by tuning into our "inner voice," which connects our "true self" to that energy of the universe that is called "God." From this center of our being we touch others, not to help them, which implies an unequal relationship where one person gives something to another that he or she is lacking, but rather as equals, in order to teach each other what we need in that moment to facilitate our growth.

I was beginning to have a broader view of the "spiritual" nature of life, and it wasn't so far out or flaky as I had thought most of my life. I was finding a center of understanding and power that acted as a steadily-growing guiding light as I continued my search for myself.

I finally read the actual books that constitute *A Course in Miracles*, and although I still felt turned-off by the explicit Christian symbolism, I was profoundly moved. I had the same feeling as when I had read Jampolsky's book on love, a disturbing yet exciting feeling that all of what I had come to see as "true" was only illusion and the "God is love" fairy tales of illusion might turn out to be the truth.

I'd always wanted a special relationship, someone to go through life with, but the *Course* suggested that this too was an illusion of the ego, the biggest illusion of all for most of us. It was the ultimate seduction of believing that our own inner separation could be overcome by joining with our lover. But that kind of joining presupposes a lack of something in ourselves, something missing that we have to get from another. What makes our lovers so important to us is that they're seen as having the key to our wholeness. Love is always provisional.

We *do* love them when we feel we've been given what we think we need, and then we fall out of love when they don't give to us in the ways we want. What this "special-woman" fantasy hides from us is our fear that there is nothing outside ourselves that really completes us, and that ultimately we are all alone. But it also hides from us the joy that in our "aloneness" we have everything we need, and by connecting with this aloneness we connect with a larger reality of God.

The "religious" words, including "God," still made me uncomfortable, but beyond the words was a reality I was beginning to experience and which was becoming increasingly clearer.

I felt I had come full circle in my search to be a "real man." I had gone on a long journey and had returned to where I had begun. It all began with memories of my father and ended with a story I read to my own children recently called "The Velveteen Rabbit." One day a young toy rabbit asks the Skin Horse, who has been around the nursery quite some time, "What is being real? And does it hurt?"

"Sometimes it hurts," said the Skin Horse, for he was always truthful, "but when you are *real* you don't mind being hurt."

"Does it happen all at once, like being wound up," he asked, "or bit by bit?" "It doesn't happen all at once," said the Skin Horse. "You become. It takes a long time. That's why it doesn't often happen to people who break easily, or have sharp edges, or who have to be carefully kept. Generally, by the time you are *real* most of your hair has been loved off, and your eyes drop out and get loose in the joints and very shabby. But these things don't matter at all, because once you are *real* you can't be ugly, except to people who don't understand."

Epilogue

The only way I can describe meeting and growing to love Carlin is to say it was subtle. There was a definite attraction at first, but it was like no other attraction I'd ever had with a with a woman. Every other relationship I'd ever had started out with a bang. The sexual energy was always strong, almost like electricity between us. With Carlin it was different. There was a deep knowing when we met that I almost didn't recognize. If she hadn't taken the initiative, I'm not sure we would have even gotten together. In the past, I had always been the pursuer in my relationships. I saw someone I liked and I went after them. I never knew if they had noticed me first because I was so busy moving in. This time, it was a new and nice experience to know I was wanted.

Although the attraction was gentle, it was also exciting and passionate. It took me awhile to realize that the difference between my feelings for Carlin and my feelings towards other women in my past was the difference between an attraction based on love and one based on fear.

All my life I had been drawn to people who reflected what I felt was lacking within me, although I never realized it at the time. The attraction was based on the fear that I would remain "incomplete" without them. The "bells and bongs, electricity and blind passion" was the energy of a man thinking he'd found the fountain of youth or the treasure of Sierra Madre. But what did we feel when we contacted another person from a position of wholeness, where there was nothing we felt we were missing? We found no flashing neon lights, just the quiet, pure gentle light of unconditional love. It was a new feeling for me.

There was nothing we needed from each other. We seemed to just enjoy the gentle flow of a mutual energy that seemed to have no beginning and move toward no end. A writer and therapist named Shirley Luthman (*Collection 1979*) described that feeling well:

> "When two people meet who have learned to balance and express their own female and male energy nothing 'begins or ends with a bang'. Energy builds and you learn to trust and appreciate that continuity and harmony so that you can feel very deeply and yet not cling or fear loss."

In the three years Carlin and I have been together our lives have merged and grown. We each feel pretty complete as people and recognize that we each have male and female, ying and yang, in our being. We've found we can love each other without so much fear. We can give because we feel full and overflowing, not because we must give out of guilt or in order to keep the other person close to us. On some very deep level we know that we cannot find happiness from the other person, but still must find it within ourselves. It's a real joy to share our lives in such a gentle way.

We still run into our fears and jealousy, still battle shadows from our past. We haven't found that perfect mating where we can sit back and rest on our enlightenment, coasting gently into nirvana. Life at times is still a bitch, but there's more humor in it than there used to be.

Carlin's son, seven-year-old Aaron, has lived with us from the beginning and my ten-year-old daughter, Sandy, moved in with us last summer. It has been a stretch for us all to merge our lives and our households.

We did a meditation together shortly after we met because we weren't sure about our desires to help raise each other's children. In the process we both became clear that we'd been parents in the past at a time in our lives when we were much less comfortable with ourselves and hence with our kids. We felt we now had another chance to give our love to a child without the fears that had dominated our earlier lives. Aaron has been a real gift for me. He's so easy to love. My bond with Sandy continues to grow. She reminds me of my need to feel a consistent flow of love from the center of my being.

Carlin's older sons, Dane and Evan, visit once in a while and my son Gene spends summers with us. Our family is large and complex, so different from the small, simple family I grew up with. In all its complexity there is a calm that enables us to continue to grow.

I like the description that John and Antoinette Lilly give of their relationship in their book, *The Dyadic Cyclone:*

"The center of the cyclone is that quiet central low-pressure place in which one can learn to live eternally. Just outside of this center is the rotating storm of one's own ego, competing with other egos in a furious high velocity circular dance. As one leaves center, the roar of rotating wind deafens one more and more as one joins the dance. One's centered thinking-feeling-being, one's own Satoris, are in the center only, not outside. One's pushed-pulled driven states, one's anti-Satori modes of functioning, one's self-created hells, are outside the center. In the center of the cyclone one is off the wheel of Karma, of life, rising to join the Creators of the universe, the creators of us. The dyadic cyclone is the combination of two personal centers. It (for us) is the male and female combination — two rotating cyclones with their enclosed centers, one rotating to the right and other rotating to the left. Is it possible to merge two centers, two cyclones, one male, one female, in such a way that there can be a rising, quiet center shared by both?"

As Carlin and I continue our process together we are finding our own answer, our own form of quiet at the center of the cyclones. The peace we have found within seems to radiate out to our work, our friends, and others whose paths we cross.

I often think about something the psychologist, Carl Jung, taught: he believed that early in most relationships men project their feminine side onto their wives, and women project their masculine side onto their husbands. He felt a person's task in life is to withdraw those projections and integrate those masculine and feminine sides into one's own personality. Carlin and I are beginning to find the peace which comes from that kind of integration.

Interestingly, our views on sexuality have changed markedly since we've been together. We both feel more secure about ourselves than at any time in our lives. Now, at this time, we agree that we could probably handle and enjoy being sexually open with others without the terrible strain we have felt so often in the past. Yet we've found, with somewhat of a chuckle, we have no interest in being sexual with anyone but each other. Although we cherish our freedom to spend time with other friends, we find our own shared intimacy and love grows best as we explore ever deepening levels of monogamy.

Although we've felt "married" for quite awhile, until recently we had no desire to formalize our union. Gradually, over a long period, we decided to "do it." We're leaving soon on a cruise to the Caribbean and have arranged to get married in the Virgin Islands. The whole process, place, and time seems just right for us. We'll have a big party for our family and friends when we get back.

The process of becoming continues. I'm not sure what the next chapter in the process will be. For now, I will end this written story and return once again to living my becoming. Writing and sharing my being with you, those of you who read this book, has been a beautiful completion for this stage of becoming my own man. I hope I have

helped you in some way to find more of a peaceful balance
within your own world, and helped you let go of some of
your isolation and open yourself more to your own beautiful being.

Jed Diamond
San Rafael, California

People Who Have Touched Me Deeply Through Their Writing

Robert Bly   *The Man in The Black Coat Turns*, 1981 Doubleday
John Enright   *Enlightening Gestalt: Waking Up from the Nightmare*, 1980, Pro Telos, Mill Valley, California
Jack R. Gibb   *Trust: A New View of Personal and Organizational Development*, Guild of Tutors Press, International College, San Diego, California
Herb Goldberg   *The Hazards of Being Male*, 1977 New American Library
Gerald Jampolsky, M.D.   *Love Is Letting Go of Fear*, 1979 Celestial Arts
Elizabeth Janeway   *Man's World Woman's Place*, 1971 William Morrow
Elisabeth Kubler Ross   *Living With Death and Dying*, 1981 MacMillan
Bob Larzelere, M.D.   *The Harmony of Love*, 1982 Context Publications San Francisco, California
Shirley Luthman   *Collection 1979*, 1980 Mehetabel & Company, San Rafael, California
Hugh Prather   *There Is A Place Where You Are Not Alone*, 1980 Doubleday & Company

Other People Who Have Touched Me Through Their Writing

George Bach & Peter Wyden   *The Intimate Enemy: How to Fight Fair in Love & Marriage*, 1981 Avon
Donald H. Bell   *Being a Man*, 1982 The Lewis Publishing Company
Jolan Chang   *The Tao of Love and Sex*, 1977, E.P. Dutton
Sukie Colegrave   *The Spirit of the Valley: The Masculine and Feminine in Human Consciousness*, 1979, J.P. Tarcher
Terry Dobson   *Safe and Alive*, 1981, J.P. Tarcher
Warren Farrell   *The Liberated Man*, 1975 Bantam
Anna K. and Robert T. Francoeur   *Hot & Cool Sex*, 1976, A.S. Barnes and Company
Betty Friedan   *The Second Stage*, 1981 Summit Books
Foundation for Inner Peace   *A Course in Miracles*, 1975 Coleman Graphics
Germaine Greer   *The Female Eunich*, 1971 McGraw-Hill
Willis W. Harman   *An Incomplete Guide to the Future*, 1979 W.W. Norton
Sam Julty   *Men's Body's Men's Selves*, 1979 Dial Press

Carl G. Jung *Memories, Dreams and Reflections,* 1963 Pantheon

Sheldon Kopp *If You Meet the Buddha on the Road, Kill Him,* 1972
    Science and Behavior Books

George Leonard *The Transformation,* 1972 Delacorte

Daniel J. Levinson, et. al, *The Seasons of a Man's Life,* 1978 Knopf

Robert A. Lewis, Ed. *Men in Difficult Times,* 1981 Prentice-Hall

Rensis Likert *The Human Organization,* 1967 McGraw-Hill

John Lilly *The Center of the Cyclone,* 1972 Julian Press

Gene Marine *A Man's Guide to Women's Liberation,* 1973 Holt, Rinehart,
    and Winston

Abraham Maslow *Psychology of Science,* 1966 Harper and Row

Deena Metzger *The Woman Who Slept With Men to Take The War Out of
    Them,* 1978 Peace Press, Los Angeles, California

Pierre Mornell *Passive Men and Wild Women,* 1979 Simon & Schuster

Jack Nichols *Men's Liberation,* 1976 Penguin

Bill Olin *Escape from Utopia: My Ten Years in Synanon,* 1980 Unity Press

Nina & George O'Neil *Open Marriage,* 1972 M. Evans

Robert Persig *Zen and the Art of Motorcycle Maintenance,* 1974 William
    Morrow

Ram Dass *Grist for the Mill,* 1977 Unity Press

Robert Rimmer *The Harrad Experiment,* 1967 Bantam

Mike Samuels, M.D. & Hal Bennett *The Well Body Book,* 1973 Random
    House

Virginia Satir *Peoplemaking,* 1972 Science and Behavior Books

Will Schutz *Profound Simplicity,* 1979 Joy Press

Merle Shain *Some Men Are More Perfect Than Others,* 1973, Charter
    House Books

Gail Sheehy *Passages: Predictable Crises of Adult Life,* 1978 Dutton

Daisetz T. Suzuki *Zen and Japanese Culture,* 1959 Princeton University
    Press

Shunryu Suzuki *Zen Mind, Beginner's Mind,* 1970 John Weatherhill
    Inc.

Alvin Toffler *Future Shock,* 1970 Random House

Andrew Weil, M.D. and Winifred Rosen *Chocolate to Morphine:
    Understanding Mind-Active Drugs,* 1983 Houghton Miffin

Ken Wilber *No Boundary: Eastern and Western approaches to Personal
    Growth,* 1979 Zen Center of Los Angeles

About the Author

Jed Diamond, a licensed therapist, has been working with individuals and couples over the past 17 years. He has been actively involved with men's groups for the past 8 years, has been on the faculty of a number of California colleges, and with his wife Carlin has led highly successful workshops in California and Oregon. His three children range in age from 7 to 13. He has published a number of professional papers. This is his first book.